'Rich with ideas and examples, Birkinshaw and colleagues have served up a practical, readable aid for managers. While I take issue with their theses that creating new businesses is a capability that can be learnt and that all companies should do it, any manager interested in growth will value this book. Rather than offering simplistic or idealistic solutions, the book provides practical guidance for the organic development of new businesses.'

Andrew Campbell, Director,
Ashridge Strategic Management Centre

'Venturing at Roche has been successful on many levels. It, along with internal Research & Development and Mergers & Acquisitions, has become one of our three pillars to drive innovation. We have used the process to rapidly screen a large number of business opportunities and fast-track the ones that promise to create the most value for Roche. Venturing has become one of the cornerstones of our strategy and as a valuable side effect we have been able to incorporate learnings from the venture process into our core business with positive results.

Inventuring provides a useful tool for evaluating whether venturing will create value for your organization and offers useful advice on how to get started.'

Heino von Prondzynski, Head of Roche Diagnostics,
Member of the Executive Committee of
F. Hoffmann-La Roche Ltd

Inventuring

[handwritten signatures]

Inventuring

Why Big Companies Must Think Small

William Buckland
Andrew Hatcher
Julian Birkinshaw

The **McGraw·Hill** Companies

London · Burr Ridge IL · New York · St Louis · San Francisco · Auckland
Bogotá · Caracas · Lisbon · Madrid · Mexico · Milan
Montreal · New Delhi · Panama · Paris · San Juan · São Paulo
Singapore · Sydney · Tokyo · Toronto

The *McGraw·Hill* Companies

Inventuring: Why Big Companies Must Think Small
William Buckland, Andrew Hatcher and Julian Birkinshaw

0077103793

Published by McGraw-Hill Professional
Shoppenhangers Road
Maidenhead
Berkshire
SL6 2QL
Telephone: 44 (0) 1628 502 500
Fax: 44 (0) 1628 770 224
Website: www.mcgraw-hill.co.uk

British Library Cataloguing in Publication Data
A catalogue record for this book is available from the British Library

Library of Congress Cataloguing in Publication Data
The Library of Congress data for this book
is available from the Library of Congress

Text design by Robert Gray
Typeset by Gray Publishing, Tunbridge Wells, Kent
Printed and bound in the UK by Clays Ltd, Bungay, Suffolk
Cover design by ego-creative

McGraw-Hill books are available at special quantity discounts.
Please contact the Corporate Sales Executive

William Buckland: *To Tania*
Andrew Hatcher: *To Ruth, Maria E and Laila*
Julian Birkinshaw: *To Laura, Ross and Duncan*

Contents

FOREWORD

Why is it so crucial for companies to invest in venturing and look to develop new businesses?

The answer lies in the complexity of the business environment as well as in the continuous disruptions and innovations that challenge existing paradigms. Venturing explores new markets and evaluates opportunities for new ideas and businesses. Deliverables include not only new business creation but also basic contributions to the growth and profit of the core businesses, financial return on investment, and from possible spin offs, as well as intangible assets and insights.

But the venturing company faces challenges. How do we combine systematic processes and approaches with innovation, flexibility and minimum rules? New ventures need their own space to develop. Without their own resources, performance metrics, and distinctive organizational design, they might fail to develop the necessary entrepreneurial spirit and disruptive thinking. And the core business focus, though dynamic, can sometimes limit the exploitation of diverging or cross-business unit opportunities.

Venturing is also all about people. Everyday entrepreneurship driven by the individual employee is key. An entrepreneurial culture is critical in enabling us to move beyond our present scope to create new ideas. To be successful, entrepreneurs must have the drive to operate independently – sometimes in opposition to conventional thinking.

Business development and creation must be approached in the spirit of exploration. In a way, it is like panning for gold. A miner works hard for many years before seeing the fruits of his labour. Unlike in a more mature business where it's relatively easy to forecast results, it is difficult to set exact targets for venturing. Small innovations will be uncovered here and there, but it's hard to find 'nuggets of gold' every day. It can take years to hit pay dirt.

But with hard work and commitment, 'gold' may be discovered and the rewards can be great.

Throughout Nokia our venturing teams are constantly looking for new business ideas outside the natural development path or focus of the current activities, and we have spent a lot of time developing and refining our venturing approach. The many findings in this book not only support, but also expand on our own experience, as well as open new insights into the venturing world.

This book represents an important and timely contribution to the field of corporate venturing. Buckland, Hatcher and Birkinshaw have put together a detailed and thoughtful account of the process of developing new businesses inside large companies, and their rich examples from companies that are currently involved in venturing make the book very engaging.

If you are personally involved or interested in new business development, I encourage you to read *Inventuring*. It provides a detailed how-to guide to setting up a venturing unit, but more importantly it shows how you can turn business creation into an integrated capability and a long-term source of competitive advantage.

Pekka Ala-Pietilä
President, Nokia

PREFACE

Corporate entrepreneurship is a controversial subject that evokes widely different responses from business executives. These responses tend to be quite polarized, so that at times the subject has seemed to us like a religion – either you believe in it, or you do not. For every manager who thinks that fostering new businesses ('business creation') is a central activity for any large firm, another intones the word 'dotcom' and rolls his eyes. For every executive that says, 'Seems obvious', another asks, 'Isn't it the same as Army Intelligence?'.

We don't think that corporate entrepreneurship is a religious practice open only to the initiated. Nor do we think it is an oxymoron, or that at root it has much to do with dotcom. Instead, we consider it to be no more and no less than an important business discipline (albeit a complex one), like strategy and any branch of commercial law. However, there are few books about corporate business creation and fewer business school courses. There isn't even an agreed-upon definition of the term 'corporate venturing'.

We have written *Inventuring*, and set up the companion website at www.inventuring.com, to convince executives of the perennial value of business creation, to demystify the subject and help end its long history of coming into and then going out of fashion, with all the excess, wastage and lost opportunities that this has entailed. With our detailed analysis, we aim to enable every major firm to make business creation part of its core business practices.

ACKNOWLEDGEMENTS

The summer of 2002 was a good time to be writing a book about entrepreneurship in large corporations. Business schools and coffee shops were crawling with business development executives and corporate entrepreneurs ready to talk about their experiences. The majority still working seemed to sense that their numbers had been dwindling, and were friendly and helpful.

We are grateful to the 80 or so executives who have helped us with our research, many of whom cannot be named, and to others who have helped and inspired us. We would like to thank Philipe Agard, Judith Allen, Andrew Barker, Nick Basing, Rob Batenburg, John Bates, Harry Berry, Heather Bewers, Beverly Bittner, Stephen Brandon, Nick Brooks, Chong Su Kiong, Phil Colman, Sir Peter Davis, Stuart Degg, Cliff Detz, Karen Donoghue, Erik Findeisen, Vince Forlenza, Tim Forrest, Gerd Goette, David Guermeur, Jon Hanley, Jan Harley, Mike Harris, Adrian Hennah, Keith Hollender, Joran Hoff, Neil Hood, Tim Jones, Tim Keating, Rob Kirschbaum, Mark Klopp, Petra Koselka, Susan Lambert, Carol Lauffer, Paul Lee, Terence Lyen, Matii Malka, Rupert Markland, Markku Maula, Anne Miller, Andy Morrison, Gordon Murray, David Norgrove, Duncan Norris, Raphael Offer, Michael Pearson, Pekka ala Pietila, Owain Powell-Jones, Victor Prodonoff, Heino von Prondzynski, Martin Purves, Alyson Reed, Seth Samir, Rene Savelsberg, Nikolai Schleip, Johan Schmid, Hollie Schmidt, Peter Schmidt, Francois Scolan, Aamir Shah, Lonnie Shoff, Simon Spurr, Quentin Solt, Kalyan Sundaram, Brian Sutphin, Petteri Terho, Tom Uhlman, Tomas Ulin, Dietrich Ulmer, Erik Vollebregt, Robert Walker, Rick Wills, Philip Wilson and Simon Yun-Farmbrough.

Finally, we would also like to thank our reviewers, Andrew Campbell, Clark Gilbert, Keith Macbeath, Patrick Regner, Carsten Thode and Jose Santos, and our editors at McGraw-Hill, Elizabeth Choules and Sarah Butler.

1 Introduction

Picture the following scenario. The busy executive flies into Heathrow Airport on a Virgin Atlantic plane. After a quick shower in the arrivals lounge, she takes the Heathrow Express train service into the city. On the 15-minute journey she first calls the office on her Ericsson phone to tell them she is on time for her 10 o'clock meeting. Then she gets out her IBM laptop, hooks up to the Internet, and orders some groceries from Tesco.com for delivery that evening, paying with her Egg credit card.

Does anything strike you about this scenario, apart from the rushed lifestyle of this hypothetical executive? There is one theme common to all of the products and services that the executive used in this short period of time. *All of them are new businesses created within existing companies.* Virgin Atlantic was a new business created within Richard Branson's media empire. The Heathrow Express was completed in the late 1990s by BAA, the company that runs Heathrow Airport. Ericsson's handset business grew out of the company's network infrastructure business. IBM's PC business was newly created back in 1981 when the company focused on mainframes. Tesco.com is a free-standing business unit within UK retailer Tesco, while Egg is an online retail financial supermarket spin-out from UK-based financial services firm Prudential.

This may not seem unusual. Surely it is the job of existing companies to create new businesses – to find new ways of meeting their customers' needs, and to create value for their shareholders? But, the fact is, most companies have varied histories in the creation of new businesses. In many of the cases mentioned, there was internal resistance to the new business idea, and widespread scepticism in the marketplace before the business took off. Think back, for example, to Richard Branson's original announcement in 1984 that he was going to launch an airline. Few believed it would last for a year, and yet 18 years later it is a successful, entrenched business.

The venture paradox

While researching this book we became fascinated by the paradoxical nature of business creation – we call it the *Venture Paradox*. Big companies apparently hold all the cards – money, people, marketing, brand, technologies – when starting new ventures. Even during the heyday of business formation in the late 1990s, many start-ups only became commercially viable through the power and scale of large firms. For example, Cisco became famous for aggressively buying up any new technologies in its heartland and plugging them into its growth engine. Charles Schwab moved decisively into online broking once it realized how popular E-trade was becoming, and has prospered.

Consider three powerful contemporary technology and market developments, although there are plenty of others: renewables in the energy industry, online banking in personal finance, and online distribution in the music business. Start-ups cannot readily address the business opportunities inherent in these developments, firstly because the assets required to address them are vast, and secondly, because incumbent businesses in those industries have those assets. Only companies such as Shell, BP and ExxonMobil can undertake renewables. Only a firm such as Prudential, with sufficient capital reserves, can set up an online bank, while the example of Napster shows us the huge advantages of incumbent firms, however conservative and monolithic, in the music business.

These opportunities are, like the organizations best positioned to exploit them, huge. When fully developed they require the scale capabilities – global brands, multinational logistics, great pyramids of skilled staff – that large firms possess. On the surface, then, the match is excellent. However the exploitation of any business opportunity starts with a series of small actions – one manager writing an email to another, an informal meeting to frame the questions, some 'seed' money dug out of R & D budget, a cheap-and-cheerful prototype with no back-end. This small-is-beautiful approach, otherwise known as the *start-up*, provides the flexibility, creativity and readiness to advance, that is fundamental to all business creation. However, it sits at odds with the organizing principles of large firms. Senior executives deal with governments and financial markets rather than small venture teams and with budgets of billions rather than hundreds of thousands. As a result, small projects looking into big ideas get pushed down the organization structure to managers focused on operations and profit and loss who are ill-equipped to manage them. Conversely, when a firm decides to 'do venturing', the favourite approach is to throw tens of millions at the problem, form a specialized unit and announce it to the markets with a fanfare.

Consequently, most large firms have great difficulty coping with the new business models which technology and market changes produce. They have trouble giving such opportunities the necessary levels of management attention, and they struggle with the appropriate organizational arrangements. However, while the problems are significant, they are by no means insurmountable. There are many firms in such diverse industries as power (UK utility Powergen), medical products (Switzerland-based Roche Diagnostics) and consumer products (Diageo) working hard at business creation through a carefully managed venture development process. Others, including Nokia, Shell and New Jersey-based Becton Dickinson, manage their business creation activities on a more integrated firm-wide basis.

SCOPE AND POSITIONING

Inventuring describes why firms should use business creation for corporate growth and renewal and provides a detailed guide to how a business creation capability can be built and sustained. By using a wealth of examples from a wide variety of big firms that have managed to think small, we disentangle fact from fashion and the good from the mediocre, and offer executives a comprehensive guide to the strategic uses and management of business creation.

We should establish at the beginning that we see business creation as a *business development technique* which can be used on business opportunities both inside and outside a firm's core business, such as Heathrow Express (outside) and Tesco.com (inside). It sits alongside three other business development techniques: acquisition, corporate venture capital and business extension. We see business creation (which we also call *venturing*, to avoid thrashing the term to death) as the neglected sibling in this family, and part of our mission is to correct what we see as a major deficiency in contemporary business development.

The book extends the thinking of two recent works. Gary Hamel's *Leading the Revolution* put forward the concept of an internal market in ideas, people and capital and pushed the agenda for business creation. While we do not entirely buy Hamel's concept of an internal market, we strongly endorse his belief in the centrality of business creation to corporate success. This book extends Hamel's work by providing a detailed 'how to' guide to the art of business creation that helps firms incorporate the market in their business development activities, where it belongs, while isolating day-to-day operating activities from its effects.

Inventuring can also be seen as an extension of Clayton Christensen's *The Innovator's Dilemma*, which shows how disruptive technologies destroy firms and outlines briefly how to resolve the dilemma. Again, we endorse Christensen's main argument that disruptive technologies should be separated from the mainstream businesses if they are to survive. But we also move this line of thinking forward, by showing how it is possible to achieve separation within a more integrated approach.

It is important to explain what this book is *not* about. Firstly, it is not about corporate venturing *per se*. While the term 'corporate venturing' has many different uses, we define it as the pursuit of growth opportunities *outside* a firm's core business using either business creation or corporate venture capital. Corporate venturing's use of the business creation technique has led some executives to conclude that they are one and the same. They are not. Business creation is a technique in its own right while corporate venturing is the use of either of two techniques in pursuit of growth.

Secondly, the book is not about corporate venture capital. This technique involves *buying* a stake in an external business for financial or strategic purposes. Business creation, by contrast, involves *building* a business either wholly inside the firm or in alliance with another firm. Although firms buy and build businesses for broadly similar purposes, the mechanics of buying a business have little in common with the mechanics of building one.

Business creation and the dotcom era

When a storm is raging, the best advice is to stay inside, batten down the hatches, and sit it out. However, once the storm has passed, you can begin to take stock of where the damage was done – you can plot the path of destruction, and evaluate what survived and what did not.

In the last few years business creation has become associated with the dotcom era, and writing this book provides us with an opportunity to take stock of those years – the period from 1995 to 2001 when the rise and fall of the technology, media and telecoms sectors became an obsession. Many companies got caught up in a bubble economy in which capital was abundant and good business ideas scarce. Then as the boom turned to bust, the market dynamics were inverted, and many solid business ideas found themselves fighting for capital from highly sceptical investors. We think of it as a vast natural experiment. What sort of conclusions should we draw from it?

First, and regardless of the number of established firms that got their fingers burnt, the dotcom era underlined the importance of investing in business creation. The Internet was a classic disruptive technology, and as such it was either a threat or an opportunity, depending on the flexibility and openness to change of the incumbents it affected. Some firms were slow to react, and allowed upstarts to muscle their way in – think of the established players in book retailing, travel agency, and stockbroking. Others moved more quickly, and turned the power of the Internet to their advantage – think of Microsoft, Reed Elsevier in information services, and Merck-Medco in drug retailing. In these and many other industries, the need for established companies to invest in new products and new business models was undeniable. It is an obvious point, but one that is missed by the many firms that have closed down their loss-making venture units in the last couple of years.

Second, the basic laws of economics around new business development still hold. The many ill-thought-out business models and get-rich-quick schemes that surfaced in the late 1990s were eventually put to the sword, while those ideas with true value-creation potential have for the most part survived. Equally important, the companies that made money out of new business creation during this period were the ones that retained their investment discipline and diligently screened the thousands of proposals they received, put together high-quality management teams, refused to throw good money after bad, and managed their exit. In short, the companies that knew what they were doing profited. Many corporate investors, who arrived late at the party with no underlying competency in business creation, paid the price.

Third, the dotcom era underlined the different qualities of the 'open market' and the large firm as arenas for economic development. The vast majority of the new business concepts emerged in the market – often in Silicon Valley, but also in dozens of other hotspots around the world – but most became commercially viable only through the power and scale of large firms, as with Cisco and Charles Schwab. The market and the large firm are, in other words, complementary to one another. Economic growth is fuelled by the symbiosis between them, not by one or the other alone. This underlines the need for bridging mechanisms between the two – venture units and the like – even if they are hard to manage.

So the trail of destruction after the storm – the remains of Enron, Marconi, Worldcom, and thousands of long-forgotten dotcoms – tells us only part of the story of the dotcom era. Equally important are the things that survived – the ongoing need for business creation, the demand for disciplined investment and business-building skills, and the symbiosis between the market and the firm. These are the enduring lessons of the dotcom era, and the principles on which we build in this book.

THEMES AND ORGANIZATION

Inventuring has four principal themes. First, when used effectively, business creation is a tool of great *strategic and financial value* for firms wrestling with the twin problems of growth and renewal. Second, business creation is a *capability* involving skills and staff across the firm which takes time to build up and requires careful management if it is to survive the ups and downs of corporate life and deliver to its full potential. Third, business creation is *by no means easy*. In most firms entrepreneurship is haphazard and *ad hoc*, and few of those who try to systematize it have succeeded in the longer term. Fourth, the firms that have succeeded in building and sustaining the capability have done so not through specialized venture units but by *integrating* it into their processes and their business culture (even though the ventures themselves require separation), with the result that using it has become routine and unexceptional. Let us consider each of these themes in turn.

Business creation delivers strategic and financial value

The six examples that we mentioned at the beginning (Virgin, BAA, Ericsson, IBM, Tesco and Prudential's Egg) have all been successful[1] for their parent firms and in several of them the venture propelled the firm in a new strategic direction. In each case the parent chose to create a separate business to follow up the opportunity it had identified. And all six involved the parent firm using its existing assets to get into the business opportunity, in conjunction with new assets that it developed or bought for the purpose. For example, BAA owned an airport with poor public transport and knew hardly anything about railways when it embarked on its joint venture with state-owned British Rail. But it does now: the Heathrow Express has set new standards in UK public transport. Prudential used its reputation and capital to secure the banking licence that it needed and then Egg developed the customer interface and service model itself.

At this stage (this is the last of our definitions) we should say that in *Inventuring* we use the term 'assets' in its broadest sense to describe what a large firm has and a start-up does not. Our definition includes tangibles such as offices, factories, staff, patents and customers and intangibles such as relationships, brands, processes, knowledge, capabilities, competences and experience.

Business creation is particularly important for companies that are facing disruptive changes in their environments. Christensen focuses on the threat posed by disruptive technologies and the new business models that start-ups deploy to exploit them. Equally important, we argue, are market changes driven by demographic factors such as increased wealth, changing attitudes towards the environment, generational change, and political and regulatory factors. These factors have a profoundly disruptive influence on incumbent businesses. For instance, a combination of regulatory and wealth effects led to the advent in the US, and now Europe, of low-cost airlines with a series of cost innovations that have dramatically altered the shape of the commercial airline business and threatened its incumbents.

The technique of business creation, when used effectively, enables a company to reinvent and adapt its core business by exploiting the opportunities that these new technologies and market changes bring, and thereby helps executives to sustain the value of the firm. Business creation is the means by which large businesses with real assets – firms in drinks, automobiles, mining, power generation, oil, banking and so on – adapt those assets to a changing environment and thereby reinvent themselves.

Looking at the examples that we started with, we can see that business creation also enables a company to extend its strategic assets by expanding incrementally outside its core operations into adjacent areas where those assets are relevant. Prudential set up Egg – an online bank – internally, while Ericsson moved along the mobile telecommunications value chain into handsets. Moving into an adjacent business is not substantially different from adapting an existing business to disruption: the same technique of asset adaptation and extension is required.

Business creation is a capability

The companies that made money out of ventures during the dotcom era were predominantly the better venture capitalists, not large companies. The reason for their success can partly be explained by the fact that they were early into the game, but the more fundamental driver is simply that they knew what they were doing. There is a skill to investing in and nurturing new businesses, and it is a skill that most large companies have never developed.

Many of the big failures, such as the example of Kudu recounted below, can be attributed to a lack of systematic capabilities in business creation. Venturing involves staff across the firm, investment and support at a corporate level, and new systems for selecting ventures and processes for developing them that take account of their inherent risk and uncertainty. Venture-building is a craft that requires a wide range of skills including all those taught on an MBA programme plus sales, project management and advanced corporate politics. Indeed, one executive told us that developing his venture had been, 'an MBA every day'.

Business creation capabilities exist at a number of levels. Individual managers must have the experience and skills to identify and nurture promising opportunities. There is need for a business creation *process*, usually at the level of the venture unit, to filter out unattractive opportunities and add value to the more promising among them. Finally, there is need for a firm-wide capability to support new business creation, even when it cuts against the priorities of the mainstream business.

The role of business creation capabilities is played out in Chapters 3 and 4. We show that these capabilities are continuously evolving, and that an important success factor is recognizing one's own strengths and weaknesses in this area.

Business creation is difficult

It is no secret that business development – in all its forms – is difficult to do well. Most acquisitions end up creating no value for the acquiring company, while corporate venturing (as we define it) has had a mixed level of success over the years. Even new product development within the core business can be risky. This book is accordingly dotted with (mostly disguised) examples of failure – nearly as many as there are successes. But as Keats observed, 'Failure is, in a sense, the highway to success, inasmuch as every discovery of what is false leads us to seek earnestly after what is true.' Like Keats, we are not afraid to use failure as a way of defining and illustrating what is good.

In June 2001 the opportunity arose to meet 'Gavin Smith', a disaffected former employee of Anglo-French media company Kudu. Smith had a fascinating story to tell. A story of greed, hubris, and ignorance, and ultimately a loss to the company's shareholders of £100 million.

Kudu was a fast-growing media company with strong brands and high-quality content. In 1999, under pressure from the stockmarket, Kudu created a new business group – Kudu Ventures – with a fund of £100 million and a free mandate to build a stable of online businesses. The executives running Kudu Ventures were under enormous pressure. The parent company had committed to revenues of £150 million within 3 years, and a 30 per cent internal rate of return. Therefore, they knew they had to act quickly. For the first few months, they 'just gave out the money' to anyone with an Internet project. They hired consultants to put technological infrastructure in place and plundered the parent company for any start-up businesses with an Internet theme.

Four employees in late 1999 grew to 450 people by mid-2000, when Kudu Ventures had 38 businesses in its portfolio, two-thirds with full funding and one-third still at seed-funding stage. Gavin Smith was brought in to value these businesses. He found 'hastily-written business plans, completely unrealistic revenue targets, and no truly transformational ideas'. Equally worrying for Smith, there was no portfolio approach, because every business was making the same assumptions about Internet growth. They would all succeed, or they would all fail.

By early 2001 it was clear that the businesses were nowhere near their revenue targets. Smith started to challenge the growth projections, but his comments and those of outside consultants fell on deaf ears. Finally in June 2001, with losses mounting and pressure now coming from the parent, Kudu Ventures laid off 150 people, including Gavin Smith. Another round of layoffs in late 2001 saw Kudu Ventures wound-up with essentially no new businesses to show for the £100 million it had invested.

Gavin Smith's experiences at Kudu Ventures highlights two of the tensions inherent in business creation. First, start-up ventures can benefit enormously from linkages to the parent company, and ultimately their value to the parent depends on the strength of those linkages. However, too many linkages too early can do irreparable harm. Kudu Ventures never broke free from the tyranny of its parent – targets were imposed from above, with little thought as to whether they were realistic, and investment decisions were subject to internal review. Also, many of its businesses were constrained by the existing identities of the brands they were leveraging.

The second tension is that while venture units do not always work they are an important, even critical, step in the development of a business creation capability. Venture units can combine the large-firm attributes of size, reputation and experience, and the small-firm attributes of flexibility, speed and entrepreneurial thinking. But some end up with the bad qualities of both large and small firms. They do not have the hunger and the street-wisdom of true start-ups, the connections and capabilities of large firms or the independence they need to provide consistent direction to the ventures under them. Consequently, while venture units and other hybrid structures can be successful, it should be no surprise that many of them fail.

In sum, the process of business creation involves the managing of so many tensions that the results are often disappointing. But, given the strategic importance of business creation, our approach is to work on the things you have to do to get it right, rather than to dwell on the risks.

Business creation should be integrated on a firm-wide basis

While the venture unit is the most common structure for facili-tating business creation, we prefer to see it as a means and not an end. The long-term successes are the firms that have realized that business creation does not take place exclusively in a venture unit. Instead, they see business creation as a much broader capability that is integrated into their corporate make-up. At UK retailer Sainsbury's, for example, CEO Sir Peter Davis chose not to create a venture unit when tying existing venturing activities in to the group centre in 2001. Instead, he created a virtual group called 'Reinvent', composed of senior executives from around the company, whose job was to look for ways of regenerating and growing the core business. This involved creating new businesses, but his personal support for the project made it possible to integrate it within the strategic planning process, so that staff are now more prepared to take risks. Mike Harris, who worked with Davis at Prudential when developing Egg and who is now respon-sible for Egg's own business creation activities, says, 'Most of the best ideas come from inside the business. We don't have a venture unit though. Instead we have a strategy function which looks at ideas. Sometimes it takes on its own projects, and others it just assists and sponsors.'

There are a number of other examples. A senior executive we spoke to at Hewlett Packard commented that the company 'no longer had a venturing activity'. Instead, HP had integrated it into the strategic planning process, so that, for example, an investment in a promising start-up would still be made, but only if it fitted with the 5-year plan of a particular business unit. Nokia still has a major venture unit – Nokia Ventures Organization – but its success has made it a centrepiece of the company's growth strategy, rather than a sideshow. Other companies, including Shell and Becton Dickinson, have developed an integrated approach to business creation. There are also a few large corporations that have retained their entrepreneurial culture, including 3M, Virgin and Racal. Here again, business creation is integrated into the core of the company, rather than being seen as something marginal.

The idea that business creation should ultimately be integrated into firm strategy is central to this book. In Chapter 4 we define three business creation *modes*. The first is *Ad Hoc*, where business creation happens occasionally through the efforts of the entrepreneur who succeeds despite, not because of, the system. The second is *Focused*, a system-based approach that relies on a dedicated venture unit to develop the capability. This approach can be highly effective, but it is vulnerable to changes at the top of the company and in the broader business environment, so that most venture units end up lasting for no more than 3 or 4 years. The third mode is *Integrated*. Here, business creation is more deeply embedded into the corporate culture and has a much broader level of support than in the *Focused* mode. The final two chapters of the book examine the elements of the *Integrated* mode in great detail.

THE STRUCTURE OF THE BOOK

Inventuring is divided into three sections. Section 1 (Business creation and the firm) addresses the broad strategic agenda of the firm and the role that business creation plays within that. In Chapter 2 we look at the need for growth and renewal in established companies, and the different business development approaches that can be used to achieve these twin imperatives. Business creation, we argue, is far less well understood than acquisition, corporate venture capital and business extension, yet is at least as important.

Chapter 3 focuses on the phenomenon of business creation – how it usually happens, what sort of companies are good at it, and what conceptual approaches are typically used to make sense of it. We then develop our 'business creation model' to show how the appropriate approach to business creation varies with a firm's existing capabilities and its opportunity set. A business creation audit tool is provided to help executives assess the position of their own companies on the model.

Chapter 4 looks at the dynamics of business creation using the model developed in the previous chapter. We describe how many companies develop and then lose their capabilities in business creation. From this analysis, we deduce three distinct *modes* of business creation and how firms move between them. Finally, we show that an *Integrated* firm is best placed to overcome the difficulties of business creation and exploit its inherent value.

Section 2 (Developing a business creation capability) is the longest section in the book, consisting of eight chapters, and provides a detailed how-to guide to the development of a business creation capability. Chapter 5 describes the basic business creation architecture: the elements that have to be put in place to support the development of new business ideas. Chapters 8–11 describe the core activities in venture development: Sense, Start, Seed and Set-up. Chapters 6 and 7 examine the two overlays: the process for selecting ventures (Chapter 6) and the support activities offered by the venture unit (Chapter 7). Figure 1.1 illustrates this overall structure.

Finally, in Chapter 12 we turn things around to look at the role, demands and activities of the corporate entrepreneur. This is a stand-alone chapter, but it provides an important perspective that

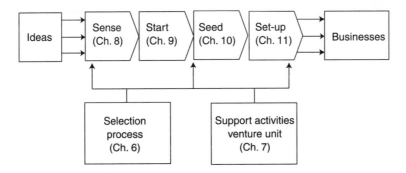

Figure 1.1 Business creation architecture

is complementary to the main thrust of the book, the rest of which is written from the senior manager's point of view.

Section 3 (Integrated business creation) moves back up to the level of the firm to consider how an *Integrated* business creation capability can be built. Chapter 13 takes a broad look at the key factors separating the successful and the not-so-successful firms in terms of capability. Chapter 14 looks at some examples of companies that we believe have developed an *Integrated* capability, including Nokia, Shell and Becton Dickinson. We end this chapter with the common elements that underlie this model.

NOTE

1   We should acknowledge that Ericsson's handsets business is no longer a success story. However, it is worth remembering that during the first half of the 1990s Ericsson was second only to Nokia in this market and unambiguously a success.

Section 1

Business Creation and the Firm

2 The Challenge of Growth and Renewal

GROWTH

Boots, the healthcare retailer, has been a mainstay of the British retail sector for 40 years. It is consistently profitable, but has essentially stopped growing. Sales of £5.022 billion in 1998 crept up to £5.226 billion in 2001, an annualized increase of around 1 per cent. Its share price reflects its image as a reliable and mature company, with a p/e ratio hovering around 11. Little wonder, then, that the emphasis of CEO Steve Russell's strategy statement in 2002 was top-line growth: 'The focus has now shifted to achieving top-line growth through developing new products, improving the shopping experience, driving retail excellence and developing the services offer.'

Why does Boots need to grow? Part of the answer is the company's share price. A growth rate of 10 per cent per year would result in a rerating of the shares to the high-teens and a near doubling of Boots' share price. There is also a host of other reasons: more exciting opportunities for employees, a better selection of products and services for customers, and an opportunity to promulgate Boots capabilities and values into new markets.

However, there is a counter argument as well, namely that Boots has developed a strategy and organization that are ideally suited to healthcare retailing, and any attempts to grow away from that niche would detract from its true *raison d'être*. Top-line growth initiatives, according to this view, are highly risky. And they are not even in the interests of shareholders, who value Boots as a 'pure play' healthcare retailer, not as a company that fritters away its free cash flow on uncertain new ventures.

The pros and cons of corporate growth have been debated for decades, and Boots is just one of many companies that faces the dilemma of how much it should push for growth. A large part of the debate centres on the often divergent needs of management and shareholders. The focus here, however, is explicitly on the managerial agenda – on the pressures faced by top executives to grow the business, on the challenges they face in delivering growth, and on the strategies and pathways they pursue.

The pressure for growth

Every public company is under considerable pressure to deliver growth and profitability. Some observers blame the stock market for the apparently short-term behaviour it induces in executives. We may not like short-term thinking, but it is so deeply interwoven with all the other parts of the Anglo-American capitalist system that it cannot be meaningfully separated. Capitalism is built on a number of basic principles: the survival of the fittest, the freedom of individuals to act in their own self-interest, the customer's freedom to choose, and so on. These basic principles have many desirable outputs, such as economic growth, innovation and choice, and they also have some less desirable side-effects, including big wealth differentials, occasional bubble markets, an excess of lawyers, and short-term thinking.

So it is certainly true that an active capital market puts executives under enormous scrutiny, and it pressures them to put in place strategies for growth. However, at the same time, it is never a sufficient reason to push for growth. Executives understand how the capital markets work, and they know better than to bite the hand that feeds them. They have to work out how to manage the expectations of everyone with a stake in their company, and they know that if they push the growth game too far for its own sake, they will eventually get caught out. Clive Thompson, Chairman and CEO of Rentokil Initial, became known as 'Mr 20 per cent' in the European financial markets because he always delivered 20 per cent earnings growth – until the day he didn't, at which point Rentokil's shares were hammered and much of Clive Thompson's good work was discredited.

Rather than blame (or credit) the capital markets for driving corporate growth, it is useful to take a closer look at the strategic imperatives that companies face. Three generic situations can be identified, arrayed along the typical S-curve of a firm's lifecycle (see Figure 2.1).

Rapid market growth

The majority of high-growth companies, from Dell to Cisco to Nokia, are simply successful players in rapidly growing markets. These are companies that, through good luck or careful planning, find themselves well-positioned in a niche market that begins to grow rapidly. In such a market, growth is not only the obvious

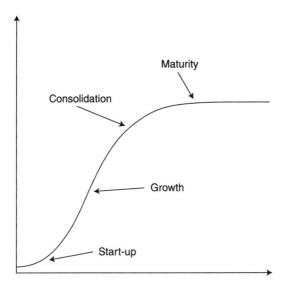

Figure 2.1   The company lifecycle

strategy, it is also easy to achieve. Of course, it can be taken to extremes. Many of the dotcoms adopted a 'get big fast' strategy without figuring out if they had a profitable business model. For example, as of mid-2002, Amazon.com had still never turned an annual profit, and it is widely considered to be one of the better bets in the dotcom sector.

Industry consolidation and industry convergence

As industries begin to mature, they typically go through a process of consolidation and convergence. This happened in the PC industry during the 1990s, and it is now underway in the mobile-phone industry. During a period of consolidation, the challenge facing any incumbent company is to look for ways of surviving – to become predator rather than prey. Consider FI Group, a medium-sized IT services group based in the UK (now renamed Xansa). Beginning in 1998, it embarked on a series of acquisitions to broaden its portfolio of services and to develop a stronger international presence. According to then-CEO Hilary Cropper, 'we would not be here today if we had not made these acquisitions' because the company would have been acquired. For Cropper, growth was central to the continued independence of the company she had worked hard to build for almost 20 years.

Industry maturity

Some industries, such as food and drink, utilities, and retail banking, creep along for decades with growth rates of 4–6 per cent. Typically, in such industries, a small group of key players emerges – what economists call an oligopoly. Think, for example, of the big four or five retail banks in Canada, France or the UK, or the 'Big Four' accountants, or the major oil companies. In such cases, true competition often gives way to a risk-averse game. The big players watch each other closer, they react quickly and their strategies converge. Eventually, they spend so much time watching each other that they lose sight of their customers.

So whatever the industry, and whatever the stage of development of the company, there is always a logic for growth. The pressure from shareholders is important, and the ego, greed and hubris of certain executives will always play a part in the decisions they reach. However, for tangible and valid reasons, growth is a cornerstone of a large number of corporate strategies.

The paradox of growth

Let us now add in a wrinkle to the plot. While every company wants to grow, the reality is that over the medium to long term they almost all fail. A study by Bain & Co.[1] sought to identify the companies that had achieved sustained growth (defined as 5.5 per cent real growth per year, inflation adjusted, over 10 years) while still achieving earnings at or above the company's cost of capital. Only 13 per cent of the companies in the sample met these criteria, despite clear evidence that 90 per cent of them had set themselves growth and profitability targets in excess of these numbers.

Other studies have reached similar conclusions. Peter Williamson of *Strategos* examined the number of companies in the S&P 500 and FTSE 100 with unbroken records of top-quartile shareholder returns since 1993, and found that less than 5 per cent fitted the bill.[2] A study by McKinsey went further, arguing that 'even the best run companies are unable to sustain their market-beating performance for more than 10–15 years.[3] The corporate equivalent of El Dorado, the golden company that continually outperforms the market, has never existed. It is a myth.'

These and other studies underline just how difficult it is for a company to grow consistently over long periods. There is, in effect, a paradox of growth, whereby the more a company craves growth (and tells the world of its plans), the more difficult growth ultimately becomes. High-profile cases like Enron, WorldCom, ABB (the European engineering group), P&G, Intel, and Marconi (the UK telecoms group) are all examples of this paradox.

There are several reasons why sustained growth is so difficult. First, even the biggest growth markets do not keep growing forever. Dell rode the 15-year boom in PCs, but PC growth eventually began to tail-off in the late 1990s. Nokia's apparent ability to keep expanding in an industry where every other company was falling apart finally came to an end in 2002 after mobile-handset sales stopped growing.

Second, as a company expands into new or adjacent business areas, it typically does not have all the capabilities it needs to succeed, and it faces attack from strong entrenched competitors. Lego moved into electronic toys in the mid-1990s, but it struggled to adapt its business model to compete with Sony and Nintendo and quickly scaled back its growth ambitions and decided to go back to toys, where it still held a competitive edge.

Third, complexity and co-ordination costs limit the size of any company. GSK, the second-biggest pharmaceutical company in the world, has recently broken up its R & D organization into six separate and competing units, a tacit acknowledgement that it had become too big and complex to manage as a single adminis-trative unit. Philips, the Dutch consumer electronics company, went through a radical programme of decentralization, outsourcing and spin-offs in the late 1990s, again because its internal structure had become unwieldy and bureaucratic. Finally, growth is a treadmill that gets faster and faster all the time. Ten per cent growth for a small company is a few million pounds a year. Ten per cent growth for GE is $15 billion in additional revenues. The bigger a company gets, the harder it is to find opportunities that are worth investment.

There is pressure to grow. But sustained growth is difficult. This does not mean that companies should shy away from the growth. Rather, it suggests that they need to have a more realistic understanding of their long-term prospects, and adjust the expectations of shareholders and employees accordingly. The worst-case scenario, as we witnessed many times during the dotcom era, is a couple of years of spectacular growth, followed by a year or two of desperate (and sometimes unethical) scrambling to sustain these numbers, then an equally spectacular fall from grace. Rather like Sisyphus, who was condemned by the Gods forever to push a rock up a hill, companies that strive too hard for growth should not be surprised if the rock rolls back down again or crushes them. A much better bet, to extend the analogy, is to push the rock up a gentler hill, where there is time to catch your breath from time to time.

The other point to clarify is that even if a majority of companies struggles to deliver sustained growth, that does not mean that executives should not try. Novice card players can expect to lose at the blackjack table, but the expert player can push the odds slightly in his favour by applying his intimate knowledge of the game. It has been shown that most acquisitions fail to deliver value to the shareholders of the acquiring firm, but that has not prevented highly experienced acquirers like Cisco and GE Capital from beating the odds. It's the same with growth. Most of the worst blunders can be easily avoided, and a combination of clear strategic thinking and experience can turn a risky strategy into a successful one.

RENEWAL

Every executive is aware of the pressure for growth that comes from shareholders, competitors, and internal discussions. However, there is an equally pressing, though less clearly articulated, need in many industries for renewal, for the adaptation of the company to the changing realities of its business environment. Every industry eventually undergoes a period during which its core processes and capabilities are subverted by technology or market (i.e. demographic or regulatory) change. None is immune.

The economist Joseph Schumpeter labelled this 'creative destruction'.[4] He observed that economic development takes place through a punctuated process that intersperses long periods of calm with occasional episodes of transition in which new technologies emerge that first supplant and ultimately kill off existing industries. Classically, we think of renewal as the process of reinventing a company once it has reached maturity. The reality is that creative destruction does not wait conveniently for a company to work through its lifecycle before striking. Instead, it can happen at any time. Some companies reach maturity and remain mature for decades. Construction, tobacco, and even automobile companies are still making products that would be recognizable to a visitor from the 1930s. Other companies never get beyond the growth phase of their lifecycle before encountering the next wave of creative destruction.

Christensen's account of the disk drive industry in *The Innovator's Dilemma* is worth remembering.[5] He studied five generations of technology in the industry and found that in no case did the leader in one technology successfully transform itself into the leader in the next. For companies such as Seagate, the need for renewal came every couple of years. Nokia, likewise, recognizes that mobile-handset growth is plateauing, and that it has to be on the lookout for new technologies and new product areas. In both cases, future growth will come through a process of renewal, rather than just an incremental strategy of more of the same.

And this is not just a high-technology phenomenon. In the 1970s, the creation of the small motorbike industry by Honda, Suzuki and Yamaha all but destroyed their US and European competitors, who were fixated on large motorbikes. In the UK, the arrival of McDonalds in the 1970s pushed the venerable British fish and chip shop into terminal decline. Seen from a distance, companies and whole industries are locked in a Darwinian struggle for adaptation to environmental change, with only the fittest surviving.

How should incumbent companies react to the threat of these so-called disruptive technologies? Consider the food retailing sector, which like many others is undergoing great change as a result of the emergence of the Internet as a new channel of distribution. As in so many other sectors, specialist dotcoms emerged, including Webvan and Peapod, but they failed to convince enough consumers of the value of their online-only business model and have mostly disappeared. Instead, it is the established food retailers, with their brand and logistical assets, that have emerged as being better positioned to exploit the online channel.

No one knows for sure how online food retailing will play out, but we can discern a range of outcomes. At the low end, maybe one-fifth of food retailing business will go to online by the late 2000s. At the high end, we can expect a transfer of two-thirds by the same date. Both cases represent a major customer grab, and in both we can expect a range of new marketing techniques and changes in the logistical architecture as stores mutate or close and deliveries are made from warehouses. Food retailers are likely to have to adapt their business models and practices to the new channel to such an extent that they will in effect be renewing themselves. Some will make it, others will not, and the difference between the two depends on how successfully each incumbent develops the required new capabilities in physical delivery, information systems and customer relationship management and deals with unpredictable secondary effects.

Extending the lifecycle

Figure 2.2 shows the company lifecycle model with these death or renewal pathways tacked on. Companies face the same two choices as they do with the challenge of growth. The first is to monitor and prepare, and then efficiently extend and adapt their business assets to change as it arrives. The second is simply to do what they do and let nature in the form of the capital markets take its course.

Executive management is by default obliged to its shareholders to try to preserve and increase the value of their assets as the environment changes around them rather than simply pass them on to a new owner (depending, as always, on the price). The onus, therefore, is on management to explain why it does not renew rather than to explain why it does.

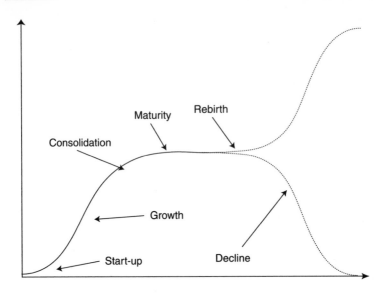

Figure 2.2   The company lifecycle revisited

STRATEGIES FOR GROWTH AND RENEWAL

The lifecycle model makes a simple and important point: whatever the industry, and whatever the stage of development of the company, there is always a logic for growth or renewal, or both. Growth comes from extending the business assets of the firm to take advantage of new opportunities adjacent to the firm's core business, whereas renewal comes through updating and reusing the assets to cement the firm in its traditional areas as technological and other changes bite.

So far we have talked about growth and renewal in a generic way. But clearly they take many forms, from acquiring an existing business, to investing in start-up ideas through to extending the existing core business. Different forms are appropriate at different times. For example, acquisition makes more sense in a consolidating industry, while organic growth is more likely in a fast-growing market. Different approaches have their own risk–reward profiles and key success factors. For most companies, the issue is not one of choosing a single approach, but of how to pull together a number of different approaches in an integrated fashion.

Consider the case of Intel which, since the 1960s, has been one of the leaders in the semiconductor industry, firstly in memory chips and then in the microprocessors that sit at the heart of the personal computer. Intel grew spectacularly through the 1990s but, as the PC industry slowed, so too did the market for microprocessors. And because of its near-monopoly in the microprocessor market, Intel was making far higher margins in that business than it could get anywhere else. The result: other business ideas, including modems and video conferencing, were starved of investment or neglected by salespeople. Craig Barrett, CEO since 1998, pointedly compared the company to a creosote bush, a desert plant that drips an oily substance, killing off all nearby vegetation.[6] He then embarked on a series of initiatives designed to push Intel in new growth areas and prepare the firm for technology change and the renewal it would have to undergo. These initiatives included:

■ The New Business Group, which invests internally in promising new technologies, including $2 billion in a web-hosting business.

■ Intel Capital, a strategic investment vehicle which makes minority investments in companies within its 'ecosystem', on the basis that increased demand for the microprocessor is ultimately good for Intel. Intel Capital has made some 500 investments over the last 10 years.

■ Acquisitions of firms in a number of related business areas, including network communications and optical electronics.

■ Selective alliances, such as a project with Microsoft to design a template for high-end cell phones including Intel chips and Microsoft software.

By the end of 2001, Intel's architecture business (i.e. the micro-processors) still accounted for $21.4 billion of its $26.5 billion revenues, and all of its profits. Many of these projects will take years before they bear fruit, but it shows how difficult and painful new programmes can be, especially in a company so dominated by a single product. But the other important point about Intel's strategy is that it is deliberately a multipronged approach. Some opportunities are best tackled internally; some can only be accessed through acquisition; others work best through Intel Capital's minority investment programme.

Business development model

Taken together, we can identify four primary methods or 'techniques' for business development as a means of achieving growth and renewal.

- *Organic business extension.* Internally generated development of new products, services or technologies that use an existing business model.

- *Business creation.* Like business extension, but involving new business models, either alone or with a joint venture partner.

- *Corporate venture capital.* Minority investments in a portfolio of relatively small companies for both financial and strategic gain, sometimes leading to acquisition.

- *Acquisition.* Outright purchase of business assets with a view to developing a new capability or entering a new market.

Figure 2.3 provides a model for selecting between these different methods[7] for any given business opportunity. It is a simplified diagnostic device which compresses the dozens of factors that affect the choice into two dimensions – the scale of the opportunity and its familiarity to the company. Nonetheless, we believe that these two dimensions capture the critical strategic choices facing a company.

The vertical axis refers to the *scale of the opportunity*, which is technically speaking the scale of the revenue opportunity adjusted for risk. The horizontal axis refers to the *familiarity of the proposed new business*.[8] Technically speaking, this equates to the proportion of assets required for successful execution of the business opportunity that the firm already has.

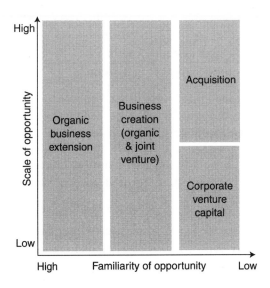

Figure 2.3   Business development model

Consider the left side of the figure first. When the familiarity of the opportunity is high, it is typically a simple extension of the existing business, regardless of whether it is a large or small opportunity. So everything from GSK developing a new cancer drug through to P&G launching a new brand of toothpaste is a business extension opportunity. Such opportunities are best handled by the existing line organization or R & D department because they fit within the prevailing processes and norms of the company.

The right side of the figure covers all those areas that are deeply unfamiliar to the company. Think, for example, of Intel getting into consumer electronics, or Ford getting into the auto repair business. One could debate whether such opportunities should be considered in the first place, but the reality is that companies frequently do seek to get into unfamiliar territory. In such cases, the best approach is typically acquisition, especially when the opportunity is big and not so risky. For smaller opportunities or those that are highly uncertain, corporate venture capital is an attractive model because it allows the company to place small bets on emerging products and technologies without the irreversible commitment of an acquisition.

Finally, the middle ground, in which the company has some familiarity with the opportunity, is the natural home for business creation. This method involves the use of some existing assets but also typically requires the development of new ones. In cases where the opportunity is relatively small, such new assets can often be built internally. In cases where the opportunity is larger and the firm wants to defray risk, or where the firm must have access to someone else's asset, such as a customer channel or a technology, business creation is often done through an alliance. Egg, which we detail below, is an example on the borderline between joint venture and organic business creation.

Because business creation sits in the middle ground, it is important to define the boundaries between it and other techniques. Let us consider each of these business development options in turn and define those boundaries.

Organic business extension

Business extension involves reapplying existing business models. It includes new features on existing products, new product lines for existing markets, and new market segments for existing products. For this reason, almost all business extension is new product development and can be undertaken within the existing structures and processes of the firm.

However, as soon as the business extension opportunity cuts against established processes it becomes difficult to manage. In Chapter 9 of *The Innovator's Dilemma*, Christensen describes the problems of developing an electric car within an existing automobile company:

> The electric vehicle is not only a disruptive innovation, but it involves massive architectural reconfiguration as well, a reconfiguration that must occur not only within the product itself but across the entire value chain. Hence, my project would need to be managed as a heavyweight team in an organization independent of the mainstream company. This organizational structure cannot guarantee the success

of our electric vehicle programme, but it would at least allow my team to work in an environment that accounts for, rather than fights, the principles of disruptive innovation.

Christensen's solution to the electric car opportunity is to conceptualize it as business creation, even though the opportunity falls well within what many would think of as the traditional core of the automobile firm. The same logic applies to all other business development possibilities that in any way challenge the standard processes in the firm. Table 2.1 lists some examples to help clarify

Table 2.1   Examples of business extension and business creation

Business extension

■   Defend existing business – new features, superior performance, higher quality. For example, Dell's new line of laptops.

■   Extend existing business – brand extensions, new product lines. For example Smirnoff Ice, a clever and successful new product.

■   Adapt existing business – entry into new markets or new customer segments. For example, Ikea's expansion into North America, or Mercedes' moving into the mass-market car segment.

Business creation

■   New business built on existing customers. Using relationships with customers to provide new sources of value. For example, Unilever's home-cleaning business called MyHome, or Tesco.com.

■   New business built on existing assets. Using existing assets or capabilities as sources of new growth opportunities. For example, BA created low-cost airline GO in the late 1990s. Easy Group and Virgin both deploy a brand and certain underlying values to get into new businesses. BAA created Heathrow Express in partnership with British Rail. GM created OnStar, a mobile telecommunications platform for automobiles.

■   New business built on existing technology. Using existing products and technologies to develop new business opportunities. For example, Ericsson's handsets business, IBM's Personal Computer business, or Mercedes investment in Swatch cars.

the distinction between business extension and business creation. Meanwhile, the concrete example of Egg shows more broadly why new business models have to be developed outside the structure of the firm.

In the mid-1990s Sir Peter Davis, CEO of financial services firm Prudential, spotted an opportunity to offer banking, mortgages and other financial services via the telephone and cut out expensive branch networks and commission-hungry independent financial advisers. In 1995, Davis recruited Mike Harris, who had built up telephone bank First Direct for Midland Bank (now HSBC), to run the venture. Like Davis, Harris felt that the time was ripe for a new class of customer-focused intermediaries to compete with the lumbering vertically integrated incumbents in banking, cards and insurance. Both men could see the Internet, and the possible reinvention of retail financial services, looming large.

Prudential Banking (subsequently Egg) was set up as a separate business unit with Harris reporting directly to Davis. 'There were four reasons for this', says Harris. 'First, big companies like Prudential have processes to stop people making mistakes, and some people within the company, especially in strategy, felt that this was a big one. Second, we did some market research and found that Prudential's brand was just not credible for such an innovative business model. Thirdly, none of this was predictable. It required a different sort of risk management from the norm, and therefore different people. Lastly, we were obsessed with customers. We did 'deep-dive' customer research and derived our strategy from it. But the idea that customers could dictate a business strategy was considered radical in The Prudential.'

Prudential entered joint venture discussions with a major UK financial brand. But, according to Harris, 'Trying to get an agreed vision and strategy was a nightmare because we had a different risk profile from them: they wanted to get more revenue from their channels with low risk. The other problem was that it was difficult to separate out the relevant activities of both companies so that neither was running the race with two horses.' In the end, Prudential decided to go it alone.

Prudential Banking quickly moved on to the Internet and became Egg. Launched in 1998 after a spend of £80 million, Egg reached its initial 5-year target of 500 000 customers and £5 billion deposits in 6 months, and is now a financial services supermarket, offering loans, insurance, mortgages, credit cards and funds in addition to banking, as originally envisaged by Harris and Davis. After an IPO in 2000 – to 'institutionalize its independence', according to Harris – Egg broke into profit in the fourth quarter of 2001 and reported pre-tax profits of £9.4 million on revenues of £79.6 million for the third quarter of 2002. With 2.4 million customers, Egg's market value in October 2002 was £1.1 billion, and it is set for expansion into France in 2003.

Mike Harris, now Executive Vice Chairman responsible for strategy and new ventures, says, 'Egg's success is due to its being set up as a separate operation. Prudential was a conservative, solidly-managed company, and no way would Peter Davis have got that idea done inside the company.'

Business extension is an important development method, but is inherently constrained by the nature of the opportunities that it can handle. Indeed, one of the most common problems we see in large companies is that they attempt to manage relatively unfamiliar opportunities through their standard structures. This creates tension between profitable existing activities and loss-making new projects. Worse, it risks the application of an existing business model to the new opportunity. We call this syndrome 'subject think' – analysing the opportunity not in its own terms but through the prism of the firm's attitudes and knowledge, and addressing the opportunity with the firm's assets rather than with those that are actually required for successful execution.

Acquisition

There are plenty of circumstances where acquisition makes perfect sense. It offers speed of execution for larger business opportunities that would take time to develop in-house, and helps achieve an instant capability in, for example, a new technology or a channel into a new market. For example, McDonalds recently bought 33 per cent of Pret A Manger, a high-end sandwich and coffee chain based in London. McDonalds' strategy here is clear. It wants to use its assets (global reach, purchasing power, and capabilities in retail site development) to help Pret A Manger roll out its concept around the world.

However, acquisition is a seductive technique whose virtues for hard-pressed management often cause it to be used inappropriately. It helps executives avoid the pain of building the equivalent business themselves, it is perceived to deliver results quickly, and the cost can be capitalized on the balance sheet rather than treated as an expense. For many executives, eagerly attended by service providers operating on contingency, acquisition is the nearest and simplest lever to hand when the investment community clamours for action. As such, it can become a reflex, a habit or even a disease.

For example, in June 2002 Pfizer announced an agreed takeover of Pharmacia. Hank McKinnell, CEO of Pfizer, made the usual comments about the extraordinary prospects the merger offered, the complementary product lines, and the opportunity to create a true world leader in the pharmaceutical industry. However, within a week, Pfizer's shares had fallen 20 per cent, and most dispassionate observers were seeing the merger as a sign of weakness, not strength. What the pharmaceutical industry needs, observers argued, is new drugs, new ways of fighting disease and new ways of servicing the needs of patients, and there is no evidence that the combined Pfizer–Pharmacia can do this better as one entity than as two.

Acquisitions suffer from other disadvantages compared with business creation. Firstly, they are easy at first but difficult later whereas business creation is difficult at first but easier later. Secondly, many acquisitions fail to deliver their potential because of the years of infighting that follow the deal. They often end up pushing together two companies with water-and-oil type differences in culture, resulting in mass desertions of talented employees. Thirdly, most acquirers end up paying far too much, irrevocably, for their target, so that even if the acquisition is ultimately a success the shareholders may not see any net benefit. Business creation offers both lower costs (naturally, given the earlier stage of entry) and an approach that allows an easy exit and a gradually escalating commitment.

We could go on, but our position should now be clear: companies that are serious about renewal and growth cannot rely solely on acquisitions to do the job. Yes, they represent an important part of the growth portfolio, but they should never drive out the organic process of business creation.

Corporate venture capital

This is a specialized method of business development. The most common approach is to set up an arms-length venture capital fund, which takes responsibility for investing in, managing and exiting new businesses within a particular technology area. Sometimes these funds are wholly owned by the parent company; in others, additional partners are introduced. Either way, the objective of the fund is typically to focus on delivering financial returns. At the same time, though, the intention is to provide strategic value to the parent company, either by providing a window on new technologies or by helping to grow the 'ecosystem' of customers, suppliers and partners around the parent company's main products. Intel Capital, for example, invests in start-up companies that will increase demand for its microprocessors.

Corporate venture capital was highly fashionable during the peak years of the dotcom boom, but it has become noticeably less popular of late. However, it is still actively pursued by a number of companies, including Siemens, Nokia, France Telecom and Intel. It tends to be most useful in a time of great technological change, because it offers a way of making small bets on a variety of new technologies that the company may want to pursue.

In our view, corporate venture capital can be a highly effective approach to business development, but it is difficult to do well, and it is highly susceptible to the state of the capital markets. It is also no substitute for organic business creation, because the objective is typically to spin the new businesses off, rather than bring them inside the firm.

Business creation

We are not blind advocates of business creation as the solution for every business development problem under the sun. Instead, we would argue that the appropriate approach depends entirely on the scale and familiarity of the business opportunity in question, as defined in the business development model. Business creation makes sense for those opportunities in the middle ground that use some existing assets and whose business model does not fit neatly within the dominant structure of the firm. We would argue, however, that many renewal and growth opportunities (in some cases, necessities) sit squarely in that middle ground.

In Chapters 5 and 7 we show that a sustained business creation capability costs a few million dollars per year, barely more than a couple of medium-sized management consulting engagements. But developing this capability, as we see with Kudu in Chapter 1 and Cyntec in Chapter 13, takes time. Executives, therefore, cannot expect to 'magic it up out of thin air' when disruptive technology or market changes produce suitable renewal and growth opportunities.

In our view, firms should retain a business creation capability in all normal business circumstances. In the few short periods when nothing is happening (in how many industries does nothing happen?), the capability has an insurance value that easily justifies its cost. When opportunities that require the firm's assets do arrive, business creation is indispensable.

CONCLUSION

In this chapter we have made seven major points about firms and business creation:

■ Firms follow an S-curve lifecycle from start-up, through growth, consolidation and into maturity.

■ Growth and renewal can become imperative at any point in this cycle. Stock markets pressure firms to grow, while technology and market changes can disrupt a firm at any point in its S-curve.

■ Growth and renewal strategies involve business development – the use of the firm's business assets to exploit new business opportunities.

■ Business development is composed of acquisition, corporate venture capital, business creation and business extension. The best method for any given opportunity depends on the opportunity's scale and familiarity.

■ These four techniques have their advantages and disadvantages. Acquisition, while appropriate in some circumstances, is seductive and overused. Corporate venture capital is useful in times of rapid technological change.

■ Business creation is appropriate for opportunities with some unfamiliarity or uncertainty in the business model.

■ Because business creation is a capability that takes time to build, and because the need for growth and renewal can strike at any point, large firms should retain a business creation capability at all times.

NOTES

1   Zook, C. and Allen, J. (2001) *Profit from the Core*. Cambridge, MA: Harvard Business School Press.

2   Williamson, P. (2002) Strategy decay. In: J.Birkinshaw et al., *Future Models of the Multinational Enterprise*. Chichester: J. Wiley & Sons.

3   Foster, R. and Kaplan, S. (2001) *Creative Destruction*. Cambridge, MA: Harvard Business School Press.

4   Schumpeter, J.A. (1934) *The Theory of Economic Development*. Cambridge, MA: Harvard University Press.

5   Christensen, C. (1997) *The Innovator's Dilemma*. Cambridge, MA: Harvard Business School Press.

6   *Business Week*, 13 March 2000.

7   Note that this model is similar to one proposed by Robert Burgelman. See Burgelman, R.A. and Sayles, L.R. (1986) *Inside Corporate Innovation*, New York: The Free Press.

8   The dimension of familiarity is also related to the concept of a *disruptive technology* as popularized by Harvard Professor Clay Christensen. A disruptive technology is one that ends up cannibalizing an existing business area, but because it initially offers a lower price–performance ratio than the existing technology it is of limited interest to the company or its existing customer base. We prefer the term familiarity (or rather unfamiliarity) because it is much broader – it includes any novel new business venture that may or may not impinge on the company's existing revenue stream.

3 Business Creation Today

Let us move down from the broader strategic imperatives of the firm to the specifics of business creation. This chapter describes some of the different approaches to business creation that we have seen in practice, and it provides a way of thinking through the approach a particular company should take.

EXISTING PRACTICE

For many companies, business creation is not a legitimate or recognized activity. It typically happens haphazardly, through the sporadic efforts of entrepreneurial individuals who have a good idea and then push it through despite the efforts of the system to kill it. However, a minority of companies has moved beyond this approach to something more systematized. Let us make some broad observations about how business creation typically occurs in practice, before describing our model.

Business creation can occur anywhere inside the firm

The first point is that new businesses can potentially come from anywhere. Some parts of the organization are more likely to breed new businesses than others, but experience suggests that it is important to cast the net fairly widely. Table 3.1 identifies six possible locations where business creation could occur, ranked in increasing order of effectiveness.

Table 3.1 Locus of business creation in the organization

- *The line organization.* Responsible for making and marketing existing products and services to existing customers. Almost by definition, the line organization is not suited to business creation, but paradoxically most of the good ideas originate there. So one option, as we will discuss in greater detail later, is for the line organization *also* to take responsibility for creating new businesses.

- *R & D unit.* Responsible for the systematic development of new technologies and products. Funding and priorities are usually provided by the existing business units and at corporate level.

- *Business development unit.* Responsible for charting medium- and long-term strategic options for the company, and making investments to support them. Acquisitions and alliances are a major part of the typical business development unit's work, but it is also involved with business creation. Business development units generally report to the top executives.

- *Venture unit.* Responsible for investing in and developing small businesses with potential strategic benefit to the company. Depending on the company, the venture unit may be closely tied to the business development unit, or managed as a completely autonomous entity.

- *Special project unit.* A one-off or short-term unit established to pursue a specific corporate objective. For example, the coffee and tea division of Sara Lee created a programme called *Decathlon* in the mid-1990s to work up a set of new business ideas to deliver the CEO's ambitious growth objectives. While this programme operated rather like a venture unit, it was designed to have a limited lifespan.

- *Skunkworks.* A special-purpose entity formed to protect and nurture a specific new business opportunity. A skunkworks is never a formal organizational unit – it is created using bootlegged funds, typically with a senior sponsor who ensures that other senior executives turn a blind eye to it. Part of the appeal and success of skunkworks is that they operate as illegitimate units.

At one end of the spectrum, the line organization and the R & D unit are designed around the existing products and services of the company. As such, they are perfectly geared to extending the existing business, but less well suited to business creation. At the other end of the spectrum, the skunkworks and the special project unit are created explicitly around the need for business creation. In the middle are the business development unit and the venture unit. Generally speaking, the venture unit has greater freedom in decision-making than the business development unit, so it is positioned closer to the skunkworks and special project unit. However, both have the capacity to deliver both business extension and business creation.

These different organizational locations are often used in combination. Consider, for example, Volkswagen's development of the New Beetle in the period 1993–1998. The New Beetle began as 'Concept 1' in a classic skunkworks project housed in Volkswagen's Simi Valley, California, design studios. After generating enormous public interest at the Detroit Auto Show in 1994, it was taken on by the business development group at headquarters, and once they established its viability it was passed on to the R & D group for development and design. By the time it reached the market in 1998 it was owned by the line organization.

This process of evolution is fairly typical. The idea of a New Beetle was surprisingly radical for a big, conservative company such as Volkswagen, so it was up to the skunkworks unit, rather than the R & D organization, to establish its viability and generate customer interest. But once the idea had built support inside the company, it was sensibly turned over to the R & D organization because it represented a good fit with the existing product lines of the company.

The Volkswagen example highlights that business creation is a system-wide activity, often cutting across traditional organizational boundaries. All the different elements of the organization are needed, some at different times in the lifecycle of a project, and some for different types of projects. Even those companies that have formal venture units for pushing business creation still need to involve the line organization and R & D group in the exercise.

Moreover, most companies have so many possible loci for business creation that no one takes responsibility for the whole thing, and it often gets neglected. We talked earlier about business *extension* as a method of business development. Extension is unambiguously the responsibility of the R & D unit and the new product development process. But business *creation* often has no natural home. It is a small part of the work of many different units, so no executive is specifically accountable for succeeding (or failing) in the creation of new businesses.

Business creation is usually done better by small firms

Our second broad observation relates back to the earlier discussion on the company lifecycle that we described in Chapter 2. Simply put, a company's capabilities tend to vary with its position in the lifecycle. In the start-up phase, companies are typically highly entrepreneurial and exhibit speed, flexibility and responsiveness. In the consolidation or maturity phase, on the other hand, companies tend to have scale-based capabilities such as rolling out a product on a worldwide basis or low-cost manufacturing.

In terms of business creation, it is perhaps self-evident that genuinely new businesses tend to emerge in the world of 'open market' start-ups and not in mature companies. The standard argument is that the early stages of business creation work best in the open market system through the entrepreneurial efforts of thousands of small companies and the later stages are best handled by large companies with their superior market power and economies of scale. Silicon Valley provides the best evidence of this. New companies form all the time, each one convinced it will become the next big thing. Most of these start-ups are destined to fail, but the few that survive typically reach a point in a few years where they have to choose whether to go it alone, or whether to sell out to a big company. More often than not, they go for the big-company option, because it is the surest and quickest way of reaching the necessary level of scale.

The business creation capability of the open market is well understood. Many big firms actively seek out the rising stars as prospects for acquisition. Cisco, the world leader in networking products, has pushed this model further than most, to the extent that it often prefers to 'acquire and develop' rather than pursue its own in-house R & D. However, most large firms argue that this approach comes at too high a price, and that they need to take responsibility for their own new business development – even if their bureaucratic environment means they don't do it as well. There is also a significant trend towards doing both: retaining a strong internal new business development capability, while also acquiring and in-licencing technologies as appropriate. All major drug companies, for example, have an active in-licencing activity for buying in new compounds at various stages of development.

Some large firms have business creation capabilities that are more usually associated with small firms

The third and more radical observation is that big companies do not have to accept the tyranny of the company lifecycle. Consider for a moment the example of 3M, the famous manufacturer of Post-It Notes, Scotch Tape, and a host of other industrial and consumer products, because it highlights an important point about how capabilities vary over the company lifecycle.

On many measures 3M is highly innovative. It still generates 25 per cent of its revenues from products less than 3 years old. R & D expenditure is around 7 per cent of revenues, and the culture is highly supportive of mavericks and entrepreneurs. The company's overall growth level is less impressive, though – only 4 per cent average growth per year since 1996. Not the story one would expect from such a highly regarded paragon of entrepreneurship.

How is it that a highly innovative company can struggle to deliver top-line growth? One clue is the company's decision in 1996 to spin-off its data storage business as an independent company called Imation. As always there were many reasons for the spin-off, but the underlying logic was that the data storage business was in a mature sector with low growth prospects and was dragging down the 3M share price. The ratings of the two companies after the demerger confirms this logic – 3M's price–earnings ratio varied between 1996 and 2001 in the range 19–28, Imation's in the range 12–16. The share performance of the two companies has also diverged accordingly, with 3M outpacing Imation.

The Imation spin-off suggests an interesting hypothesis: 3M is good at managing early- and mid-stage growth businesses, but relatively poor at later-stage or mature businesses. Early-stage growth requires a heavy investment in R & D, lots of experimentation, plenty of 'slack' time for innovators, and an acceptance of failure. 3M expects margins of 25–30 per cent to cover all of these costs. Later-stage growth, in contrast, is all about operational efficiency, global roll-outs, standardized procedures and process (as opposed to product) innovation. This is a different set of capabilities from those 3M has perfected over the years. By spinning-off its imaging and disk storage activities, 3M was tacitly admitting to the capital markets that it was the wrong parent company for mature businesses of that type.

Just like every other company, 3M is good at some things and less good at others. That said, it is a large company that still behaves like a small company with the ability to conceive and develop new businesses. The downside is that it is not so good at the later stages of the lifecycle; but it is living proof that big companies can be entrepreneurial, nimble and creative.

3M is unusual, but it is not unique. Hewlett Packard used to have a similar profile, and a similar record of innovative excellence but weak top-line growth. Virgin and EasyGroup are both highly successful creators of new businesses, but through a highly decentralized model that some observers have termed 'branded venture capital'. Another interesting example of a Peter Pan company is the UK electronics company Racal, which opted to spin-off its interesting technological innovations and new business ideas, rather than attempt to commercialize them in-house. Vodafone was Racal's biggest success, spun off in 1991 and

10 years later one of the most valuable companies in the world. Racal, like 3M, realized that its strength lay in the early stages of the product lifecycle, so rather than attempt to build later-stage capabilities it spun-off its commercial successes and retained its entrepreneurial spirit.

DEVELOPING A BUSINESS CREATION CAPABILITY

These broad observations reinforce two important points about business creation. First, while it can potentially take place anywhere, it more usually takes place nowhere. Instead, the short-term demands of the day-to-day business drive it out. Second, most large established companies are simply not very good at business creation, because they focus on managing their scale-based activities.

However, this does not mean it is impossible to achieve. As Sir Martin Sorrell, CEO of media company WPP, puts it, 'every CEO wants the power of a global company with the heart and soul of an entrepreneurial company'. The benefits of being big and small at the same time are not impossible to achieve, as examples such as 3M and Racal confirm, but they do require a focused and sustained effort.

The internal market approach

How should we square the circle of business creation? What approaches should a company use to develop the capability to create new businesses without giving up the benefits of scale and scope?

One highly influential idea about business creation that has been doing the rounds is to bring market forces to bear *inside* the company. Big companies, it is argued, employ Soviet-style central planning, rather than a free market system, to allocate resources and divide up responsibilities. So, given the proven superiority of the open market system, we should rethink our top–down, bureaucratic structures and replace them with decentralized, fluid, and market-like alternatives. Reigning strategy guru Gary Hamel has argued that, 'if you want to free the entrepreneurial spirit inside your company, you're going to have to figure out how to set up and sustain dynamic internal markets for ideas, capital and talent'.[1] McKinsey consultant Dick Foster has taken a slightly different tack, arguing that long-term success is achieved only by corporations that are, 'as dynamic and responsive as the market itself'. He argues that they should adopt the principle of creative destruction – by, 'creating new businesses, selling off or closing down divisions whose growth is slowing, and abandoning outdated, ingrown structures'.[2]

Some scepticism is in order here. Hamel, Foster and others are partially right. Most big companies could do with becoming less bureaucratic and more open to new ideas. The market metaphor is, too, an effective way of thinking through some of the possible changes that could be made.

However, at the same time, the market metaphor is both misleading and dangerous. Misleading because companies are not market systems – they represent a distinctively different way of allocating resources, and they have structure and hierarchy for sound reasons. Dangerous because, if taken literally, it can do serious and lasting damage to its adherents. Enron provides the most graphic evidence of this point. It is no coincidence that both Hamel and Foster used Enron as their prime example. Enron created a market-like organization in which individuals were encouraged to pursue new ideas and were rewarded handsomely when these ideas took off. Seed funding for new projects was freely available and individuals were free to move to more exciting job opportunities within the firm. While many of these policies were sound, taken as a whole they created a system that ratcheted up the risk/reward payoffs for individuals to such an extent that people were prepared to lie, steal and cheat rather than miss their growth targets. This ultimately destroyed the company. Seldom has the term *creative destruction* been more appropriate than as an explanation for Enron's demise.

Our approach

The idea of bringing market-like systems to bear inside large companies is sound, as long as it is not taken too far. The fact is, large companies are operators rather than investors and have structure and hierarchy because it allows them to mass-produce and sell their products reliably and efficiently. Business creation is a wholly different pursuit at the opposite end of the scale requiring the tolerance and even encouragement of uncertainty and risk. Firms can be pushed to become better at creating new businesses through a more supportive culture, an openness to new ideas, a long-term commitment to growth, and so on. However, it should be recognized that attempts to change them by completely mixing operating and investing activities can only be at best partially successful.

Our approach is therefore somewhat different from Hamel's and Foster's. We believe that large firms need to acknowledge the limitations of their existing organization, culture and systems and accept that attempts to build a free-wheeling 'internal market' within their operating structures will struggle. However, we believe firms can and should graft a 'managed market' on to that structure and use it to manage their business development activities, including those inside the traditional core. Grafting, as opposed to incorporation or integration, allows the company to confine the operation of this managed market to business development and prevent unnecessary spill-over into its operational units.

It is worth spending some time on the qualification 'managed'. Take the case of Diageo's Guinness Good Times project, which we feature in Chapters 9 and 10. This is a travel business heavily dependent on the Guinness brand. Use of this brand, particularly by new ventures entering the unknown, is tightly controlled by various committees and is ultimately a significant management responsibility. So much so that the venture team had to jump through various hoops and change its business model before receiving official sanction for the project, even though the venture is relatively small.

Firms are not the same as markets because they have assets. These assets form a company's strategic context and are a powerful influence on management when devising strategy, selecting opportunities and deciding how to develop them. Virtually every project involves the use of one asset or another – any project that didn't would arguably be better off being undertaken outside the of firm or not at all. By and large, markets match money, ideas and people, whereas business development within firms matches assets, money, ideas and people. But these assets are at the same time being used by the operating business to generate financial returns. Whether and how they are available for use by ventures are complex issues that require active management.

ASSESSING THE POSITION

The second half of this chapter looks at the different approaches to business creation that a company can pursue. It is self-evident that some companies are successful at business creation while others are not. But is this because of some intrinsic difference between the make-up of the two companies? Or is it because they face different sets of opportunities? The question is analogous to the nature versus nurture debate in psychology, and as with that debate there are strong adherents to both points of view. One school of thought in business strategy focuses on the attractiveness of a given industry as the prime driver of profitability and growth. The other points to the idiosyncratic differences between companies as the key discriminating factor.[3]

We see clear support for both arguments. Consider a case such as the demerger of ICI and Zeneca (see Example 3.1) in 1993, which represents a form of natural experiment akin to studying pairs of separated twins in the field of psychology. At the outset the two firms had essentially the same capabilities, so the initial difference in their ratings can only be attributed to their different opportunity sets (Zeneca had more than ICI). But their subsequent divergence, with Zeneca far outpacing ICI in all respects, can only be explained by bringing capabilities into the equation.

This distinction between capabilities and opportunities is at the core of our analysis. In the previous chapter we explained what business creation is, and why it matters. In this chapter we now take a closer look at the prospects for business creation in different companies, and at different times. By mapping capabilities and opportunities as separate axes, we can identify four generic positions a company can occupy in terms of its business creation strategy.

Example 3.1   The demerger of ICI and Zeneca

In 1993, ICI took the bold decision to spin-off its pharmaceutical, agrochemical and speciality chemical businesses into a separate company called Zeneca. The underlying logic was clear: ICI had become too diversified to generate any meaningful synergies between its disparate businesses, and its low-margin commodity chemical businesses were stunting the growth prospects of the high-flying pharmaceuticals business. At the time of the demerger, ICI was generating profits of £487 million on revenues of £17.3 billion and its stock was trading at a price–earnings ratio of 20. One year later, the two businesses had already begun to diverge. ICI, now a chemicals and paints group, had earnings of £588 million on £11.9 billion revenues, and a price–earnings ratio of 20. Zeneca had earnings of £522 million on £4.48 billion revenues, and a price–earnings ratio of 30.

How do we explain this divergence? The beauty of a demerger is that it is a natural experiment. The two companies had essentially the same quality of people, the same systems (recruitment, rewards, IT, etc.), and even broadly similar organizational cultures. Yet within a year they were being rated very differently by the capital markets. The reason is that ICI and Zeneca faced different market prospects. ICI was stuck in a bunch of low-growth and declining bulk chemical businesses, as well as a moderately attractive paints business. Zeneca was a player in two of the hottest growth sectors of the early 1990s – pharmaceuticals and biotechnology.

However, the story does not end there. Over the next 6 years, Zeneca grew at an impressive rate, spun-off its agrochemical business and merged with Sweden's Astra. In 1998 its net earnings were £716 million on £5.5 billion revenue, with an average price–earnings ratio of 36. In 1999 the new AstraZeneca was seen as one of the more impressive players in the global pharmaceutical industry, with a better product pipeline than its competitors. ICI, on the other hand, went through a painful transformation, getting out of its bulk chemical businesses and moving into speciality chemicals through a couple of overpriced acquisitions. Its 2001 results were disappointing – £99 million earnings on £6.4 billion revenues, with a price–earnings ratio of 11. Once the bell-wether of the London Stock Exchange, ICI rated only 80th place in the FTSE 100.

Certainly, ICI dealt itself a bad hand. However, we must also conclude that it played its hand poorly. ICI had some valuable businesses, and it bought a number of others, albeit at inflated prices. It had a talented body of managers, a strong brand and a high profile. However, over an 8-year period it never managed to build the capabilities it needed for consistent, profitable growth. Zeneca, on the other hand, managed to capitalize on its opportunities and deliver double-digit growth in pharmaceuticals for 6 years, a feat that many of its competitors in the same industry could not match.

Capabilities

We have argued that the different stages of the company lifecycle require different capabilities to be managed effectively. We have also suggested that most large companies develop capabilities that make them better at managing the later stages of the lifecycle, and correspondingly poor at managing the early stages. However, this is far from being universally true, because there are exceptions like 3M whose capabilities are better attuned to the early or middle stages of the lifecycle. Such examples provide inspiration and hope to others.

What are the capabilities a company needs for business creation? The earlier discussion has mentioned some of them, but taking a broader perspective, we find it useful to group them into three categories:

- *Resources*. A company needs to have specialized and high-quality resources to enable business creation, and a cadre of dedicated people who are experienced at identifying, funding and developing new business ideas, as well as killing off those that do not meet their targets. The firm needs technological capabilities and equipment so that individuals with good ideas can realize their potential inside the company. It needs a good network of contacts with suppliers, customers, partner firms and venture capitalists, and entrepreneurial and skilled individuals who can take an idea and run with it.

- *Systems*. The systems inside the company have to support and foster business creation. The company needs a capital allocation system that makes it relatively easy to get access to seed funding, and provides multiple possible sources. The incentive and reward systems should stimulate initiative, and encourage individuals to turn their ideas into new businesses. The reporting structures should be simple and non-bureaucratic. The support systems should enable the sharing and cross-fertilization of ideas.

- *Culture*. The organization culture should be supportive of business creation. There should be an openness to new ideas, and a dislike of the 'not invented here' syndrome. The culture should be tolerant of well-intentioned failure, while at the same time seeking out and rewarding high perform-ance. The culture should also value collaborative and helpful behaviour among employees.

Example 3.2 is a self-assessment audit of business creation capabilities, divided into the above three categories. Executives can rate their own companies by answering the questions and following the instructions afterwards.

Opportunities

While capabilities are the indispensable resource of business creation, the opportunity domain that the company faces also plays an important role in shaping the appropriate business creation strategy. It is important to recognize that opportunities are not equally distributed across the different sectors of the economy, as illustrated by the ICI–Zeneca case study in this chapter.

How can we identify the underlying opportunity domain facing a company? There are a number of tangible and relatively objective elements: think of measures such as the aggregate growth of the market, the global scope of the market, the potential for disruptive technological and market change, or the emergence of new competitors. Example 3.3 is a brief self-assessment audit of a company's opportunity domain. This should be completed in the same way as Example 3.2, the capabilities audit.

However, there is a slight problem with this approach as opportunity, like beauty, is in the eye of the beholder. For example, where one person sees a mature industry, another sees a renewal opportunity. In one well-known study, John Stopford and Charles Baden Fuller examined the fate of some 80 companies in mature industries.[4] All faced broadly similar opportunity domains, but 12 of them were able to look beyond the obvious (and depressing) characteristics of their market and identify areas for growth and renewal. To use a more recent example, the UK fast-food industry looks mature and overcrowded to most observers, but two entrepreneurs, Julian Metcalfe and Sinclair Beecham, still managed to identify an opportunity for a chain of upmarket fresh sandwich shops called Pret A Manger. This harks back to our earlier point about disruptive market change. In the fast-food industry, nobody is safe from the effects of increasing incomes and corresponding changes in taste.

Opportunities need to be perceived to be valuable. The companies that perceive opportunities are those that have developed the capability to do so. It is an internal characteristic of the company, not an inherent feature of the industry in which it is competing.

As such, the ability to perceive opportunities really belongs in the *capabilities* section. This is the reason why in the self-assessment audit we restrict ourselves to relatively objective measures of industry and market growth.

The Business Creation Model

Capabilities and opportunities come together into what we call the 'Business Creation Model', shown in Figure 3.1. Using this, it is possible to identify four generic approaches to business creation that companies use. Later in the chapter, we present an audit tool that makes it possible to determine where a company sits. That said, the model does not explain the strategies that firms should follow. Rather, it describes the strategies that firms *are* following.

Companies with weak capabilities and unattractive opportunities are choosing to *Evade*, while companies with strong capabilities and good opportunities are in *Emphasize*. Those with strong capabilities and unattractive opportunities are electing to *Ease* up

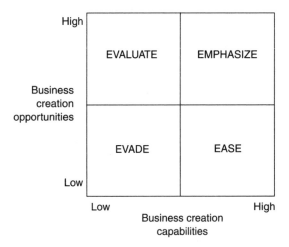

Figure 3.1   Business Creation Model

on business creation in the (probably temporary) absence of any uses for it. Lastly, companies facing attractive opportunities but which have weak capabilities are in *Evaluate*. The latter is the most difficult box in the model. What happens when a firm faces a great range of opportunities? It can ignore them or it can start to develop them. Both of these different approaches fit within the *Evaluate* quadrant, a conundrum with which we deal in the next chapter. In the meantime, we have named the box after the more positive of these two approaches.

This model serves two important functions. The first is simply as a means of categorizing different companies, on the basis that companies with the same positions on the business creation model are likely to be facing similar challenges. Second, the model can be used in a dynamic way. In any given case, the strength of the business creation capabilities and the attractiveness of the opportunities will be constantly changing, so the key question for many companies will be how they move around the model. For example, are certain development paths superior to others? And how can a company best move from the *Evaluate* to the *Emphasize* box? We discuss the dynamic aspects of the model in Chapter 4. The remainder of this chapter describes and illustrates each of the four Es in turn.

Evaluate

This is a common situation in which a company faces plenty of opportunities but lacks the capability to act on them. For example, British Telecom (BT) found itself in this position during the 1990s. With its heritage as a monopoly provider of fixed-wire telephony services in the UK, BT was slow in getting to grips with the dynamics of the deregulated telecoms marketplace (though not as slow as many of the other incumbent operators). However, with the emergence of new competitors such as Cable & Wireless and Vodafone in the UK, and countless others overseas, it embarked on a number of growth initiatives. These included acquisitions and alliances overseas to build up BT's international operations, but there were also several programmes concerned with organic growth. In the following chapter we look at one of these in detail, the *Brightstar* venture unit in BT's R & D organization.

Emphasize

Where a company has well-developed capabilities and attractive opportunities it has decided to *emphasize* its business creation strategy. The example of Intel was mentioned earlier as a company that has grown rapidly for many years and that has engaged in a variety of activities all designed to foster their innovativeness and ability to create new businesses. Another example is Nokia, which has capitalized on its position as the market leader in mobile handsets to build a series of venture units and related activities all intended to help it stay ahead in the digital wireless sector.

Ease

A company whose capabilities are ahead of its opportunities has adopted a strategy of easing off (but not stopping) its business creation strategy. This situation can arise for several reasons. One is the all-too-common scenario in which a company geared up for the dotcom boom but now finds either that the new opportunities have dried up, or that it is too preoccupied with other things to pursue them. For example, Hewlett–Packard (HP) had a long tradition of technological innovation and new business creation, in large part driven by its decentralized structure that encouraged each division to behave entrepreneurially. In the mid-1990s the company tried what one executive called 'an abbreviated incubation experiment' in which it solicited ideas and funded promising business plans. This was later stopped because 'it felt too artificial'. There were some valuable learnings, but the process did not square with HP's traditional model of divisional autonomy. However, rather than give up on business creation, HP decided instead to integrate it into the strategic planning process. Each division would take responsibility for identifying its development opportunities, and then seek to address them through either organic initiatives or strategic invest-ments (with help from the corporate development group).

HP went through some tumultuous changes in the period 2000–2002, including a massive restructuring and a messy merger with Compaq, so its efforts were focused on these things rather than on business creation. Bearing this in mind, the decision to integrate business creation into the planning process (rather than separate it) was a smart move, as it provided a mechanism for building and retaining the necessary capabilities. HP, in effect, eased back on business creation for a short time, presumably with a view to re-emphasize it after the Compaq merger was completed.

Evade

Finally, there is the *evade* strategy in which a company, either tacitly or explicitly, elects not to promote business creation activities because there are few opportunities. The more interesting examples of the *evade* strategy are companies that have been active in business creation in the past, and have subsequently retreated.

Consider the example of British Airways. It was a highly successful company through the 1980s and 1990s, but through a combination of industry changes and internal problems it found itself in difficulties. BA had been relatively active in business creation. It spawned a number of foreign subsidiaries (e.g. Deutsche BA), it started GO – a low-cost airline – and it launched a number of non-airline businesses through its venture unit, BA Enterprises. These included travel health shops, an in-flight shopping business which sold its services to other airlines, and the London Eye. However, when Rod Eddington replaced Bob Ayling as CEO in 1999, he put the brakes on all these activities because there were few business opportunities inside the core (other than for a low-cost airline) and because the core was in financial trouble. He believed that his first priority was to fix this, so he shut down BA Enterprises in 2000 and sold GO in 2001. A stake in the London Eye was retained, but with a view to selling it as soon as was practically possible.

We do not want to fault Eddington's approach to business creation, because he was surely correct to focus his energies on turning around the core business. The only caveat we would add is that by shutting down BA Enterprises and selling GO, many of the relevant capabilities for business creation were lost. These are capabilities that will be needed in the future. As the HP case above suggests, a better approach that allows the company to retain some of its business creation capabilities even when opportunities are limited is to move to the *Ease* strategy.

USING THE BUSINESS CREATION AUDIT

The audit tool

The above four examples help to illustrate the four different strategies for business creation. It should be clear that we do not favour the *Evade* strategy, but the other three are all valid and necessary at different times and in different situations. Also, the business creation model is best viewed in a dynamic way, with companies moving between positions as their capabilities and opportunities change. Try to see where your own company stands now using the self-assessment audit below or you can access it online at www.inventuring.com. We have found that completing the audit takes about 30 minutes.

Example 3.2 Business creation audit: Part A

This section asks about your internal corporate capabilities for business creation.

A1. RESOURCES

1. How many new businesses with expected annual revenues of $1 million or more has your company created in the last 3 years?

None	1–2	3–6	7–14	15 or more
1	2	3	4	5

2. How big is the business creation activity (not M & A) in your company? Please indicate the <u>number of people</u> working in business creation in total in your company (not counting those working in ventures)

None	1–5	6–9	10–14	15 or more
1	2	3	4	5

3. What is the size of the business creation pipeline? Please indicate the <u>number of new business projects currently</u> being developed

None	1–2	3–6	7–14	15 or more
1	2	3	4	5

4. How many ideas are *actively* considered (i.e. one person spending at least half a day) by your company per year?

None	1–10	11–24	25–49	50 or more
1	2	3	4	5

5. How many ideas from *outside the firm* are actively considered per year?

None	1–5	6–14	15–24	25 or more
1	2	3	4	5

A2. SYSTEM

6. To what extent is there a formal idea selection system for business creation?

None	Informal	Formal 0–1 year old	Formal 2–4	Formal 4+ years old
1	2	3	4	5

7. How many ideas have been considered within this system for more than $300 000 worth of seed development funding

None	1–9	10–19	20–29	30 or more
1	2	3	4	5

8. How many ideas have been considered within this system for more than $3 million worth of investment funding

None	1–2	3–4	5–9	10 or more
1	2	3	4	5

9. To what extent is the system for selecting and developing ideas perceived to be neutral and fair?

Biased & unfair	Somewhat unfair	Uneven	Pretty fair	Totally fair
1	2	3	4	5

10. To what extent is there a formal stage or gate system for developing new ideas?

Not	Informal	Formal 0–1 year old	Formal 2–4	Formal 4+ years old
1	2	3	4	5

11. For how long, if at all, have you had a specialist business creation function?

Don't have	0–1 year	1–2 years	2–4 years	4+ years
1	2	3	4	5

12. How flexible is HR in terms of temporary assignments, non-standard packages, etc., for people working on ventures?

Never	Rare	Now & then	Flexible	Very flexible
1	2	3	4	5

A3. CULTURE

13. How senior are the executives who select ideas/ventures for development in your corporation? Please indicate the average number of levels below the CEO of the group that selects ventures.

4 levels	3levels	2 levels	1 level	0 (is the CEO)
1	2	3	4	5

14. How good a move would a well-regarded middle manager who took a job in a start-up venture generally be considered to have made?

Bad	Risky	Neutral	Good	Superb
1	2	3	4	5

15. What level of threat is there to the positions in the firm of the staff concerned if their venture is terminated?

Very high	High	Medium	Low	None
1	2	3	4	5

16. To what extent are business creation skills (market research, business & financial planning, etc.) dispersed across the firm?

None	In one place	2–5 places	6–10 places	Ubiquitous
1	2	3	4	5

17. What are the time horizons in your firm? Please select the typical time that would be considered in terms of delivering a return on investment.

1–12 months	1–3 years	3–5 years	5–10 years	11+ years
1	2	3	4	5

18. How senior is the most senior supporter of business creation? Please indicate the number of levels below the CEO.

4 levels	3levels	2 levels	1 level	0 (is the CEO)
1	2	3	4	5

19. What would happen to business creation if its most senior supporter left the company?

End	Could end	Setback	Minor setback	Nothing
1	2	3	4	5

20. To what extent is business creation connected to the other forms of business development (M & A, VC) in your company?

Not	Distant	Work together	Same top manager	Same manager
1	2	3	4	5

21. To what extent is business creation connected to corporate strategy in your company?

Not	Distant	Work together	Same top manager	Same manager
1	2	3	4	5

Example 3.3   Business creation audit: Part B

This section asks about the number and scale of the opportunities suitable for business creation that your company faces.

1. How many new opportunities ($1 million+ revenues) do you expect your industry to face over the next year?

None	Few	Tens	Hundreds	Thousands
1	2	3	4	5

2. How many new opportunities do you expect your industry to face over the next 5 years?

None	Few	Tens	Hundreds	Thousands
1	2	3	4	5

3. Estimate the rough aggregate growth potential in your industry if all the above opportunities were acted upon

0%	2–5%	6–12%	13–24%	25%+
1	2	3	4	5

4. To what extent is your industry currently subject to disruptive technological change?

Not	Low	Medium	High	Very high
1	2	3	4	5

5. To what extent does your company have under-used assets (e.g. brand R & D staff, patents, customer channels)?

None	Low	Medium	High	Very high
1	2	3	4	5

6. How much annual revenue growth is expected in your primary industry over the next 3 years?

<0%	0–5%	6–10%	11–20%	21%+
1	2	3	4	5

7. What average annual profit growth has your company achieved over the last 3 years?

<0%	0–5%	6–10%	11–20%	21%+
1	2	3	4	5

8. What is the level of maturity in your industry?

Declining		Mature		Emerging
1	2	3	4	5

9. To what extent is your industry subject to disruptive demographic, environmental, social and political change?

Not	Low	Medium	High	Very high
1	2	3	4	5

10. To what extent have new competitors emerged in your industry over the last 5 years?

No new competitors		A few competitors		Many competitors
1	2	3	4	5

How it works

The capabilities part of the audit divides into questions about resources, systems and culture. Questions 1–5 cover resources, 6–12 cover systems and 13–21 culture.

Take the averages of (a) your answers to the capabilities questions and (b) your answers to the opportunities questions.

The capabilities score is the weighted average of the three sub-scores – these weightings in effect represent the relative importance of the three elements in the overall capability. You may wish to get several people inside your company to answer the questions. If so, try to establish a collective answer to each question rather than merely average the different responses, as averaging just drives the answer for that question towards the middle of the range. The two averages define a point on the business creation model, and shows where your company is currently positioned in business creation. (For an electronic version of this audit, visit www.inventuring.com)

To illustrate the audit in action, we asked one executive in each of four firms – Shell (energy), Roche Diagnostics, Lloyds TSB (retail banking) and Kudu (media) – to complete the audit. Plotting these capabilities and opportunities scores on the business creation model shows that three of the firms are in *Emphasize* and the fourth is in *Ease*. The results are shown in Table 3.2 and Fig. 3.2.

Shell, with its long-standing Gamechanger initiative to encourage staff to create and work-up new ideas, has the greatest business creation capabilities while at the same time enjoying the fewest immediate opportunities for growth. That said, the company is likely to have to develop a long-term renewal programme in response to environmental pressure. In the near term, it closed its E-Initiatives venture unit in Summer 2002. This, according to one executive, shows that the new CEO is shifting investment capital

Table 3.2 Business Creation Model examples

Category	Shell	Kudu	Roche Diagnostics	Lloyds TSB
Resources	4.6	4.4	3.6	4.2
System	4.1	2.4	3.3	3.4
Culture	3.3	3.2	3.5	3.7
Capabilities	4.0	3.2	3.5	3.8
Opportunities	2.5	4.4	3.4	3.0

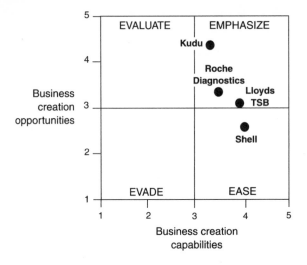

Figure 3.2 Business Creation Model examples

back towards the core business as a result more of a portfolio decision than a decision to get rid of business creation. All in all, the company has eased off on business creation in the past year while retaining the capability for the longer-term need for renewal.

Lloyds TSB is in retail banking – a mature and saturated business – and started a venture unit in 2001. According to Michael Pearson, Director of Strategic Ventures, 'the feeling was that the company could do more to generate long-term growth'. Roche Diagnostics has also started business creation within the last 2 years as one of several initiatives focused on value creation. Lonnie Shoff, who runs the venture unit, concentrated on idea generation and selection in the first instance, and is now working to improve the way that ventures are developed. Roche Diagnostics is also just starting to work with ideas from outside the company.

Kudu, the media company introduced in Chapter 1, was in June 2001 sitting on the biggest opportunity set of all, scoring five on questions about industry opportunities and underused assets. However, although it was trying to apply substantial resources, its systems were weak. As we saw earlier, the firm spent £100 million on a heap of poorly-selected and half-baked ventures, eventually shutting its Ventures unit down. The lesson from this is that applying significant resources to business creation without the necessary systems in place is a recipe for waste.

CONCLUSION

In this chapter we have made seven major points about business creation in practice today:

- Business creation can occur in various places across the firm. Typically, no executive is responsible. In this context, development of a strategic capability is unlikely.

- Firms at different points in the company lifecycle have different business creation capabilities. Mature scale-managing businesses are less competent in this area than growth businesses.

- The concept of bringing the market inside the firm is incomplete. Firms' assets constitute a strategic context. Application of these assets to ventures, in conjunction with ideas, money and people, requires a *managed* market in business development to be grafted on to a firm, rather than a market brought inside.

- Business creation capabilities consist of three underlying categories – resources, systems and culture.

- Opportunities vary by industry but are typically driven by disruptive technology and market change.

- The business creation model describes the state of a company's approach to business creation by assessing its capabilities and opportunities. Four situations – *Evade*, *Evaluate*, *Emphasize* and *Ease* – can be discerned.

- The business creation audit enables executives to place their companies on the business creation model.

NOTES

1   Hamel, G. (2000) *Leading the Revolution.* Cambridge, MA: Harvard Business School Press.

2   Foster, R. and Kaplan, S. (2001) *Creative Destruction.* New York: Free Press.

3   In the field of business strategy, there is a perennial debate regarding the relative importance of industry factors and firm-specific factors as drivers of firm performance. The former view reached its prominence through the work of Michael Porter who brought Industrial Organization economics thinking into the realms of business strategy, whereas the latter point of view has ground since through the so-called resource based view of the firm. See Grant, R. (2002) *Contemporary Strategy Analysis.* Blackwell.

4   Baden-Fuller, C. and Stopford, J. (1992). *Rejuvenating the Mature Business.* Routledge.

4 Ad Hoc, Focused and Integrated Business Creation

BUSINESS CREATION PATHWAYS

In Chapter 3 we looked at the positions of several companies on the Business Creation Model, and the reasons that they are where they are. The state of business creation within any one firm does not stay still, however. Management teams come and go, the firm evolves through its lifecycle, and the necessary financial resources ebb and flow. The result is that, regardless of the level of opportunities that a firm faces both inside and near to its core businesses, the capability of business creation is subject to a variety of drivers that in turn create it and destroy it.

Clockwise cycle

Firms move from box to box on the model, but of all the possible migration paths only a few are ever seen. We have observed that firms almost always move clockwise around it. The story of business creation in most firms that of a constant struggle to match capabilities to opportunities. For quite understandable

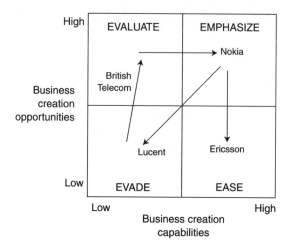

Figure 4.1 Dynamics of the Business Creation Model (1)

reasons, there is usually a time lag between the arrival of the opportunities and the production of capabilities to match. On the model, this translates into an initial up movement, followed by right, then down and then left – a clockwise cycle. We illustrate this first cycle with four examples, all drawn from the telecommunications sector (see Fig. 4.1).

Path 1. Evade to Evaluate: BT

In Chapter 3, we described how British Telecom found itself facing a number of opportunities brought on by technology change and deregulation. In 1999, Stewart Davies, CEO of BT Exact Technologies, the company's technology arm, was seeking to make the company more commercially orientated. He asked Harry Berry, a senior executive with 30 years experience in the company, to take responsibility for 'unlocking the hidden value' in the R & D organization.

Berry started to talk informally to the scientists about their ideas, and he was staggered by the inventiveness, the capability and above all the frustration of the people he met. His feedback to Davies was straightforward: 'Yes, there is hidden value in the R & D organization, and yes we can unlock it, but not with BT's money or BT's culture or BT's people.' The BT scientists lacked the basic commercial skills, he felt, to turn their technological ideas into businesses, and the standard funding process for new projects would kill off any new projects that came its way.

Berry and Davies started looking into alternative models. They quickly formed a venture unit, subsequently named BT Brightstar, and sounded-out external partners to help with funding and to provide the commercial expertise that the lab engineers were lacking. Then they began an off-beat and informal marketing campaign to shake up the traditional culture of the lab organization. Soon Berry was being inundated with new ideas.

The initial splash gave Berry enough raw materials – new ideas, exciting technologies, market opportunities, frustrated entrepreneurs – to launch Brightstar properly. External venture capitalists were called in and their expertise was used to vet the ideas and provide seed funding. Local support services were brought on-site to help with legal, accounting and financial matters. An Advisory Board of mostly outside people was created to decide which ideas were worth turning into small businesses. From its launch in February 2000 to the end of that year Brightstar launched four businesses and funded a further 11.

The early life of BT Brightstar is a classic example of the *Evaluate* strategy. First, deep environmental changes changed the opportunity set, then BT started to respond by creating an R & D-based venture unit to follow up and effectively begin the rightward movement on the business creation model. Later on, like Nokia below, BT moved to an *Emphasize* strategy.

Path 2. Evaluate to Emphasize: Nokia

The path from *Evaluate* to *Emphasize* is best exemplified by Nokia, which transformed itself over a 15-year period from an obscure Finnish conglomerate to the undisputed world leader in mobile handsets, as well as one of the leading providers of mobile networks. In the late-1990s the company recognized the need to look beyond its two core businesses, and established a separate unit, Nokia Ventures Organization (NVO), reporting directly to the President of the company. NVO quickly became an integral part of Nokia's strategic development and, as of 2002, consisted of four business development groups:

■ *Nokia Venture Partners* – an independently managed $650 million mobile communication venture capital fund, evaluated on both its financial return and the strategic exposure it provides to emerging technologies through relationships with start-up companies.

■ *New Growth Business* – a venture unit that attempts to find and develop new businesses for Nokia both inside and outside the firm. Started in 2001, it now operates over 10 ventures, ranging in venture size from five to 60 people, with another two ventures in acceleration phase with their first products coming out. It carries out large-scale, systematic idea generation using both bottom–up and top–down techniques, and recently launched a venture challenge process out of which came several hundred new ideas.

■ *Nokia Early Stage Technology* – a $40 million fund that invests in ideas of uncertain strategic value. Its approach is to set up promising business ideas as separate legal entities, and spin them in or out depending on how they evolve.

■ *Insight and Foresight* – a business intelligence operation that looks at new and emerging market and technology opportunities, typically 3 to 5 years into the future.

This list of activities is mind-boggling to most outsiders, but an important point is that it was built up gradually, with every unit filling a specific need. For example, Nokia Early Stage Technology fund was created to invest in business ideas that were not strategic enough for New Growth Business.

The four groups are managed as an integrated whole rather than a series of isolated units. This, and the direct connection to the firm's president, gives them critical mass and a much more important role in the overall strategic development of the company. Nokia also ensures that each unit focuses on its own opportunity domain, which as one executive observed, 'avoids the one-size-fits-all and fuzzy thinking of many other venture organizations'.

Path 3. Emphasize to Ease: Ericsson

Ericsson has been at the forefront of telecommunications technology since its founding in 1876. Its AXE switch was one of the first commercial digital switches, and it moved into mobile network equipment in the 1980s and then mobile handsets in the 1990s. For Ericsson, new business creation has always been at the core of its mission. As Tomas Ulin, an executive in Ericsson Business Innovation, observes, 'we have been doing this forever'.

The unit's remit is to 'produce business renewal by creating new core businesses for Ericsson, acting from another angle', and it is well established in Ericsson. Firstly, its mission is both strategic and financial – produce renewal and generate financial returns – so it is less vulnerable than it would be were its goal only one of these. Secondly, the ancillary benefits of business creation that are seen in training, recruitment and retention, PR and staff morale, are well recognized by top management. Thirdly, Ericsson's management team, including the CEO and heads of marketing, finance and technology, is Ericsson Business Innovation's governing board.

On the day before our interview with Ulin, Ericsson had announced plans to make 20 000 people redundant. Surely that meant the end for business innovation? 'No', said Ulin, 'the operation is definitely smaller. But Ericsson still has a strong desire to continue corporate innovation and the board also thinks it is necessary. Although Business Innovation may experience some downsizing, there is not much likelihood of us being terminated as we definitely answer a need in the organization and have strong support from the finance department. In fact, resistance is probably stronger in other quarters – in development, for instance, where projects are being terminated as part of the retrenchment.'

As of April 2002, Ericsson Business Innovation had around 20 active ventures and was taking forward two new cases per quarter. Ulin says, 'In the economic downturn we turned towards building and developing the current portfolio. Ericsson Business Innovation now acts as a commercialization unit, investing less on developing a new portfolio. We also look for ideas with less upfront development cost.'

It should be clear that although Ericsson decided temporarily to restrict the entry of new ideas into its development pipeline it is retaining its business creation capability through the telecommunications downturn by managing its portfolio of existing ideas. In other words, it is scaling its capabilities to the level of opportunities that it faces and thereby retaining it for the next major inflow of opportunities.

Path 4. Emphasize to Evade: Lucent Technologies

The case of Lucent Technologies is similar to Ericsson, but with a rather different ending. Lucent was formerly AT&T's equipment company, but it was spun-off in 1995 and has operated independently ever since, growing rapidly during the rest of the 1990s on the strength of its networking and transmission businesses. As part of its business creation strategy, it created two venture units. Lucent Venture Partners was an externally focused fund that took minority stakes in dozens of small start-ups, with a view to developing a strategic partnership with them and also generating a financial return. Lucent New Ventures Group was an internally-focused fund that sought to commercialize neglected technologies and ideas from within Bell Labs (similar to BT Brightstar). Both of these venture units were highly successful, and widely copied by other companies in the technology sector.

However, Lucent got into deep trouble in early 2000. A combination of stiff competition from Cisco and Nortel, a weak position in mobile infrastructure, and the beginning of the industry downturn led to a series of profit warnings, a sell-off of the stock, and the departure of CEO Richard McGinn. The previous CEO, Henry Schacht, was brought back temporarily, and he embarked on a radical restructuring, laying-off tens of thousands of employees, selling-off many peripheral businesses, and focusing on the core networking business. The telecoms slump worsened in 2001, leading to a further round of layoffs. Lucent New Venture Group was sold in late 2001 to Coller Capital, a London-based private equity company, with Lucent retaining a 20 per cent stake. Lucent Venture Partners declined to raise money for a new venture fund. Essentially, the parent company decided to get out of venturing altogether, despite its evident success in that area, to focus on reviving its core business.

INTERPRETING THE PATHWAYS

The four examples above illustrate some of the more common pathways of evolution around the business creation model. However, as the arrows on Fig. 4.1 suggest, the process of evolution is inherently cyclical, with companies such as Lucent finding themselves back down in the *Evade* box, only to subsequently move back up into the *Evaluate* box once industry conditions turn around. In fact, we can identify three distinct cycles, labelled *Focused*, *Ad Hoc* and *Integrated*.

Focused

The *Focused* cycle is by far the most common, and is similar to the classic boom-and-bust cycle often seen in the economy as a whole.

Stage one (Evaluate)

The firm moves into business creation in response to a new set of opportunities and threats. We saw that BT created a venture unit to unlock hidden value in its R & D laboratories, while British American Tobacco (see Chapter 13) set up its Imagine & Evolution venture unit in 1999 in response to a challenging presentation to the board by an IT executive.

The potential causes of investment in business creation are many: disruptive changes in technology and markets, an economic boom, or structural changes in an industry through deregulation or competitive manoeuvring. Mood helps. Business creation typically becomes fashionable at the peak of the economic cycle when investment projects are ten-a-penny and free cash is sloshing around.

Stage two (Emphasize)

Following some initial success in business creation, the firm gives the activity greater emphasis. Small experimental investments lead to much larger investments, and soon to a top billing in the firm's new strategy statement.

Nokia made this shift because of its need to keep reinventing the firm in the face of continuing technological change. Despite the downturn in the industry, it continued to emphasize business creation through the Nokia Ventures Organization. Sainsbury's, the UK food retailer, operates in a mature, competitive and saturated market and has little prospect of more-of-the-same growth. In late 2001, it formed its existing business creation efforts into its new venture unit – Reinvent – and embarked on a formal strategy to 'develop new sources of revenue through leveraging existing assets'. The result was a series of asset-extending projects based around customer demand that included a programme to open up its stores to specialist concessionaires.

Stage 3 (Evade)

The growth that sustained stages 1 and 2 eventually comes to an end, and the firm faces a downturn. This downturn causes a re-evaluation of priorities, and depending on its severity, can lead to a drastic cutting back of all activities that are non-essential to survival. Business creation, because of its front-loaded cost structure and uncertain output, is usually one of the first things to be shut down. Lucent faced collapse and concluded that business creation was a luxury that had to go. British Airways cut its business creation efforts in Summer 2001, occasioned by the arrival of new top management. The bottom line is that stage 3 often takes firms back to the beginning – to a situation in which they have neither the capabilities nor the opportunities for business creation, compelling them to start all over again.

Integrated

The second cycle is illustrated by Ericsson, which responded to the bust in telecommunications by reducing its level of activity in business creation by moving from *Emphasize* down to *Ease* (rather than to *Evade*), with the clear intention of moving back up to *Emphasize* again once economic conditions had improved. Shell continues to invest heavily in creating a 'Renewables' business (alternative forms of energy such as wind, solar, hydrogen and biomass) regardless of the ups and downs of both the global economy and the oil price, and its Exploration and Production-based Gamechanger business creation initiative ploughs on. However, in Summer 2002, Shell closed its specialist E-Initiatives unit and moved pieces of it into various parts of the firm. So, while continuing in some business areas, Shell eased off in others.

A company with highly developed business creation capabilities goes to *Ease* when the scale of profitable opportunities drops off. Economic and industry recession, the bursting of a bubble, new management or higher investment hurdles can all bring this reduction about. These drivers are the opposite of those that lead to the *Evaluate*. By moving to *Ease* instead of *Evade*, a firm retains its capabilities for another day.

Ad Hoc

Finally, there is a third cycle, *Ad Hoc*. To date, we have looked primarily at firms which have tried to develop business creation capabilities. But, other firms never try, or do try but then abandon their efforts after recession or failure. These firms sit on the left side of the model and remain largely unresponsive as opportunities come and go.

Take the case of global automobile company Belleron. Despite its vast resources this company today eschews business creation as an expensive and risky activity. In 1998 it formed a venture unit called E-Bell to take responsibility for investigating new business ideas and for introducing new Internet-style thinking. But E-Bell quickly ran into problems. The first was a strategic policy that new technologies developed in-house were for Belleron's use only, for competitive advantage reasons. This meant that business ideas requiring a development partner could not easily be taken forward. The next problem was that introducing new ideas within the firm's core automotive business was both counter-cultural and difficult because of its fixed development processes. According to one executive, 'Our systems were very controlling and prevented new business formation. We had no official mandate to circumvent them and were unable to follow a just-do-it approach. It was like extracting teeth to operationalize new companies within [Belleron].'

This drove the unit towards developing non-core ideas such as online car loans and mortgages and towards investing in external businesses. In 2000, Belleron's Corporate Strategy Group (CSG) also approached the problem. It carried out an extensive internal research programme and concluded that new technology-based customer-driven businesses could use and enhance the assets of its core automotive business. When presented with this recommendation in early 2001, Belleron's CEO said that he had no interest in internal ideas and refused funding. The result in early 2001, when the Internet boom had died down, was a decision to refocus on the core business and the end of E-Bell. According to an executive in the CSG, that was the third time that this had happened. New ventures, he says, are considered to be resource users by a company primarily interested in cost efficiency. Moreover, he says, executives think that shareholders invest in Belleron for stability rather than risk.

PLOTTING THE DYNAMICS

Figure 4.2 shows how the three different cycles can be mapped on the business creation model. From now on we refer to these as business creation *modes*. All firms are in one or other of these three modes – *Ad Hoc*, *Focused* or *Integrated* – and switch between them at points A and B. At point A the company is

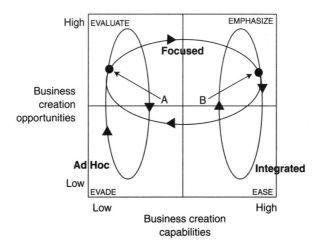

Figure 4.2   Dynamics of the Business Creation Model (2)

choosing to stay either *Ad Hoc*, like Belleron, or become *Focused*, as BT and Kudu both did with their venture units. At point B, a company in *Focused* mode is faced with adversity of some kind. It can either move towards (or stay in) the *Integrated* mode by choosing to retain its capability despite this adversity (the Ericsson example). Or it can move back towards the *Ad Hoc* mode by killing-off its business creation capability (the Lucent example).

In this view, we can see that *Focused* is the transition pathway between *Ad Hoc* and *Integrated*. In order to develop a fully-fledged business capability including suitable systems and a supportive culture, an *Ad Hoc* firm has first to get into *Focused* mode. Let us look at each of these modes in turn and define their characteristics.

Ad Hoc business creation

An *Ad Hoc* firm has low capabilities that are insensitive to its level of opportunities. The company does not attempt to develop any kind of system to direct resources to the business opportunities that present themselves. In these firms, lone entrepreneurs fend for themselves using networking and the unorthodox techniques that we describe in Chapter 12 because the culture is oppressive and there is little management support.

A great many large and mature companies stay in this mode all their lives. Such companies also feature one or more of:

■   An absence of systematic business development

■   An emphasis on operational processes and efficiency

■   A poor selection of business development method for any given opportunity

■   A preference for acquisition and alliance over internal development

For start-up companies, such failures are forgivable as they are simply too busy executing the business plan on which they were funded. Growth firms, however, face maturity in the not-too-distant future and usually need to explore different pathways. Mature firms that engage in *Ad Hoc* business creation are vulnerable both to disruptive technology and market change and to the Kudu Ventures syndrome of trying to grow the business through business creation without having the necessary capabilities.

Focused business creation

Some growth and mature companies are tipped into *Focused* by disruptive change in their industry and a subsequent urge on the part of top management to exploit it. A *Focused* firm has, or is developing, a business creation capability but has not yet integrated it into its day-to-day business development activities.

Resources are channelled to ventures centrally, possibly by a separate venture unit which acts as a capability hub. Just like the quality unit and the knowledge officer, it is blessed, and fated, with ownership of this important activity. That said, there is realistically no other way for a firm to develop the experience and understanding of how to select and develop ideas. The venture unit provides the critical mass of skills in business and financial planning, venture management, and market research, and it provides the necessary level of legitimacy for this important but poorly understood activity.

When starting out from point A on the business creation model, a firm adopts a system of selecting and developing opportunities (a venture development process) and uses its venture unit to operate it. As time goes by the selection system slowly becomes part of the firm's strategic resource allocation process. If the firm's culture is supportive and the venture unit is successful, the capability begins to disperse across business units. If not, the venture unit, and the business creation capability vested in it, are vulnerable to a blunder, a management change, operations pressure or adverse company circumstances. This then drives the company along the pathway back to *Evade*.

The pros and cons of the Focused mode

New initiatives are often killed in large companies without the top executives even knowing about it. Many argue that the agent of death is management positioned one and two levels below the top. Tim Jones, who led the development of the revolutionary stored-value card Mondex at National Westminster Bank (a UK retail bank) between 1986 and 1996, calls this the 'marzipan layer' – the level below the icing at the top of the cake. 'Life's too short to spend time with the marzipan layer if you're trying to do anything', says Jones, who managed to keep Mondex completely secret from all but a few NatWest executives until announcing it in December 1993. With their short-term P & L-based incentives and aversion to any career-threatening risk, the marzipan layer can kill business creation in an instant.

A venture unit, however, provides separation for initiatives with no guaranteed returns. In doing so, it bypasses the marzipan. In the short term, separation and critical mass are critical to success. However, in the longer term, they form a solid, concentrated target for cost cutting. Sometimes, as we saw at Belleron, political resistance in business units can force venture units into solely non-core ventures. Such units are prone to being killed-off when focus time arrives. As a result, such companies find themselves starting all over again a few years later; they get into cycles of investing in business creation, getting some successes, then closing it down and starting all over again.

Rather like a young tree that has yet fully to put down roots, the *Focused* mode is unstable and vulnerable. In Section 2 we describe a way to manage the development of the business creation capability that minimizes these difficulties.

Integrated business creation

An *Integrated* firm always maintains a high business creation capability so that it can address relevant business opportunities both inside and outside its core business. The *Focused* selection system is integrated into its strategic resource allocation processes alongside corporate venture capital and acquisition, and supporting staff are dispersed around the firm and operate the venture development process as if it were second nature. On the other hand, finance is allocated to ventures separately from operations costs, even though business creation is located in P & L-focused units. The culture is favourable because, to start with, the CEO explicitly supports venturing. Management in general tolerates risk, uncertainty and creativity, is prepared to wait for success, and helps ventures overcome middle management and other obstacles.

The difference between *Integrated* firms like Nokia and Shell and the most advanced *Focused* firms lies in the extent to which business creation fits with the firm's culture. The more business creation is culturally embedded and the more the system is a part of the culture, the greater the firm's ability quickly to scale its capability to match the level of opportunities that face it and the less it needs a specialized venture unit to grow, safeguard and deploy that capability. An *Integrated* firm, then, does not need a venture unit, although it may still choose to have one, or more.

The *Integrated* mode is half-way between the isolated venture unit model adopted by Kudu and the 'bring the market inside' model discussed in Chapter 3. The tentacles of coherent and co-ordinated 'managed market' business development spread across the firm looking for opportunities and encouraging creative thinking, to the extent that business development is pushed out to individual business units and thereby made integrated. Individual ventures, however, are still developed away from operating activities in order to safeguard each from the effects of the other.

CONCLUSION

In this chapter we have made five major points about firms and business creation:

■   Firms follow clockwise pathways around the business creation model because capabilities typically lag opportunities.

■   These pathways form three cycles. The main cycle – *Focused* – involves the firm building capabilities in response to an opportunities surge but then losing them again.

■   The other two cycles are a low-capabilities cycle – *Ad Hoc* – and a high-capabilities cycle – *Integrated*. In these cycles opportunities fluctuate, capabilities do not.

■   At any given time all firms are in one or other of these cycles, or modes.

■   Firms in the *Ad Hoc* mode waste opportunities to renew and grow. *Focused* is the transitional mode but is vulnerable. In the long term all firms should aim to be *Integrated* so that they can exploit core and non-core opportunities.

Section 2

Developing a Business Creation Capability

5 A Business Creation Architecture

This chapter describes a conceptual architecture for business creation and how to organize it. Because creating new businesses is so different from managing existing businesses, many writers have argued that it needs to be managed separately. Peter Drucker, for example, wrote in 1974 that 'the search for innovation needs to be organizationally separate and outside of the ongoing managerial business'. Many others, including Burgelman, Christensen and Galbraith, have argued for the establishment of a separate unit to cope with creative or disruptive activities.

Our position is slightly different. We see some level of separation as a necessary step for the firm to build its business creation capability and develop a track record of success. However, the ideal home for business creation is ultimately within the line organization as an integrated part of the firm's activities. The *Focused* mode is about building the capability, typically in a separate entity such as a venture unit. The *Integrated* mode is about embedding that capability firm-wide.

Think back to the days of the business process re-engineering (BPR) movement. While much of what happened under the BPR banner has now been discredited, the underlying logic was sound. It argued that companies had become organized into functional silos that completely disregarded the true flow of business processes for adding value to customers, such as order fulfilment or new product development. By re-engineering around its value-adding processes rather than its functional silos, the company would generate massive improvements in both efficiency and customer responsiveness.

Business creation can be seen as such a process – as a system of interlinked elements that draws from many different parts of the company. Conceptually at any rate, this process can be separated out from the rest of the organization. It has inputs (ideas, people, money and technology), it has processing activities (sensing, seeding, starting and setting-up) and it has outputs (typically new businesses). In the latter part of this chapter we describe the architecture of the business creation system in some detail, but before that we describe what makes business creation distinctive.

WHAT MAKES BUSINESS CREATION DIFFICULT?

Let us briefly examine the various factors that underlie the need for a distinct business creation process.

Business creation requires creativity

Business creation turns an idea into a business unit complete with staff, business plans, financial spreadsheets, prototypes and legal documents, ready for an injection of investment cash. This process requires creativity on a large scale, with the result that many entrepreneurs are driven mavericks who pay little attention to rules and regulations. Some play fast and loose with company goods and materials and use them to get what they want. They do what they have to do to develop their ventures, often within boundaries defined only by themselves.

Business creation is risky and uncertain

Tim Forrest at Powergen likes to say, 'Venturing is snakes and ladders'. In this game, players throw dice and move up a board. If they hit a snake they go back. If they hit a ladder they go forward. Games can go on for hours with no player reaching the end. Snakes infest the last few squares and long ladders dot the early ones.

Business creation is exactly like this. There is a process but, because new information arrives constantly and business models can change in an instant, this process is not linear. Some ventures fail early because of lack of revenue, others fail years later because revenues and costs are each slightly off the business case, wiping out the projected profits. Few succeed, because a venture is the aggregate of many moving parts any of which can go wrong at any time.

Business creation is complex

Business creation involves every business discipline and leads to complex cross-disciplinary interactions. The body of knowledge and skills required to produce a venture includes strategy, strategic marketing, market research, financial planning, business planning, project management, human resources, employment law, contract law, intellectual property law, technical development, operations management, negotiation, presentation, selling and corporate politics.

In each of these the devil is in the detail and, as a result, few executives are able to manage the business creation process. One venture executive says, 'It was an MBA every day. On one morning I was in front of a senior executive, writing a market research questionnaire, arguing with an IT supplier and interviewing someone for a job.' Rick Wills, an ex-British Airways executive formerly responsible for venture unit BA Enterprises, says, 'it was easier to buy a 747 than set up a new venture.'

Senior managers are ambivalent towards business creation

Senior managers are responsible for the long-term growth of the company and, as such, they should be excited about the promise of business creation. But as servants of their shareholders they are also naturally cautious about what new projects to sponsor. They end up highly ambivalent and demand a system that controls the risks and costs associated with the creation of new businesses. Stuart Degg, who set up venturing at insurance firm Royal & SunAlliance, a UK insurer, sums up senior management's attitude to cost control in ventures. 'There was a greater level of interest in smaller numbers than was typically the case elsewhere in the business.' Management wants resources applied to ventures appropriately and the ventures developed quickly and efficiently. But ventures go backwards as well as forwards and many executives view cancelled ventures as a waste of money rather than as a way to save money.

In public companies, senior management likes discipline, routine and calm in day-to-day operations. Creative activities and behaviour can be disruptive, and possibly damaging, to the firm's assets, and the last thing management wants is loose cannons. Senior managers therefore need a buffer between business creation and operations to avoid disrupting the day-to-day routine of the company.

Corporate entrepreneurs are hard to deal with

Corporate entrepreneurs (discussed in more detail in Chapter 12) need freedom to pursue their ideas without getting bogged down in the rules and constraints of a large company, while also getting resources and help from those around them. Unfortunately, their freedom to act is frequently compromised by well-intentioned but narrow-minded managers in other parts of the firm (Example 5.1).

Example 5.1 Telegene: the case of the frustrated entrepreneur

In 2000, a venture team within the main division of Telegene, a French IT services group, proposed a web-based portal for accountants. The division sold information, software and consulting services to the accountancy and other professions. The team obtained sponsorship from a senior executive in the Divisional Technology group and moved into his group to prepare a business case on the understanding that, because the executive's budget was already fixed, they would request funds from his boss, the Divisional CEO, when they were needed.

The arrangement worked well until a request to do some market research was denied on the grounds that market research is 'expensive'. The team was also told by the CEO that its product had to use unsuitable software being developed by the Division. Finally, it was ordered to concentrate on a single narrow customer segment because Strategy deemed it the most valuable. After trying to find a home somewhere else in the firm, the team broke up and one member left the company.

Michel Lefevre, the venture team manager, felt he had learned the hard way. He now has a shopping list. 'Next time I would need organized support and a guaranteed job at the same level if the venture didn't happen. I would need some kind of bonus for the value created at the venture stage, a high-level sponsor at board level and a clear idea of how long the venture would be separate from the company and how it would go back in or out. And the freedom to look for investors outside if the company didn't want to invest further at any stage.'

From this example we can distil the three basic needs of the corporate entrepreneur. If managers are to be successful with venturing then they have to understand, and plan for, these needs.

- *Freedom*. Corporate entrepreneurs need to be able to spend money, create prototypes and destroy them if they do not work, and follow their own instincts as they learn. Rob Kirschbaum of Dutch chemical firm DSM's New Business Development Group says, 'A company can kiss to death a venture by being too paternal and all-knowing. The entrepreneur must be allowed to be proud and arrogant and to ask for help himself.'

- *Resources and help*. Many ventures are started by technologists with little experience of winning investment. A venture team, like a self-formed rock group, is unlikely to have the complete set of skills required to produce its venture. Dietrich Ulmer of Siemens Mobile Accelerator, which helps external teams develop their start-ups under the Siemens banner, says, 'Corporates understand sales contracts, margins, pricing and negotiations. They can collect money and run billing systems. Ventures do not understand these things.'

- *Security*. Corporate entrepreneurs need to believe that the company will not arbitrarily steal the venture, close it or redirect staff. We have seen plenty of examples of companies that failed to provide this basic need and, as a result, bred distrust and suspicion in their employees. But, because the company holds most of the power, the entrepreneur must trust it to use that power carefully and wisely.

In *Ad Hoc* firms most corporate entrepreneurs are found in places that offer them security. They live either at the fringe of the firm where the threat to their security is weakest, or they hide underneath a friendly manager who provides cover for their entrepreneurial activities. In *Focused* firms, however, corporate entrepreneurs have a more legitimate and formal existence.

THE KEY ELEMENTS OF A BUSINESS CREATION SYSTEM

The chosen system has to respond to the unusual nature of business creation and the often-conflicting needs of the two key customer groups. There are many different models, but experience suggests that an effective system has the following key elements as a minimum:

Careful selection and planning processes

A combination of rigorous venture selection and project planning helps control risk and uncertainty. Tomas Ulin of Ericsson Business Innovation describes how the company retains control.

The environment is very demanding, and when a venture comes under the Business Innovation umbrella people and projects can fail and be shut down. We spend carefully and our staff are highly measured. Ericsson Business Innovation is not R & D, it is a commercial environment. This is the dirty world of business well away from idea Utopia and we are disciplined and creative, possibly more disciplined than an Ericsson development unit. The result is that we get things done that they can't do in corporate units. Traditional Ericsson projects can get too big and sometimes growth in the number of people involved can become uncontrolled, but we at Business Innovation impose a structure and a system of milestones which makes it easier for us to get stuff out.

A staged business development to help control costs

By dividing business development into stages with formal selection before entry into each stage, *Focused* companies such as Powergen eliminate ventures as soon as a fatal weakness becomes clear (see Example 5.2). Venture teams also carry out the cheaper tasks first, so that large expenditure is only incurred once a venture has been through several selection points and its business case is robust.

Example 5.2 Powergen (1)

On the office wall of Spark, Powergen's venture unit, hangs a picture about 5 feet wide by 3 feet high. It shows the stages of the venturing process, where the ventures have got to and how much has been spent on each to date. The picture even lists the ventures that have been stopped and how much had been spent on them. Tim Forrest is Spark's manager in charge of business incubation. 'Symbols are very important,' he says, 'we aim to create and maintain a community of people interested in venturing.'

Powergen, a UK power utility, spent the 1990s investing in the cost-effectiveness of its power operations and expanding into the gas generation and retailing markets. Over time, competition and pressure from the government regulator reduced wholesale power prices and reduced revenues in the monopoly wires business. That, and the diminishing returns available from efficiency investments, drove the CEO at the time, Nick Baldwin, to consider how to develop revenue growth and to conclude that venturing was a solution.

Previous attempts to develop new businesses within the firm had enjoyed mixed success. So, in early 2001, two strategy executives visited similar firms that had used venturing to grow the top-line. They came back with insights into how using a staged system could increase the quality of ventures selected for development and also reduce the risk of individual venture failure. The decision was made to vest this system in a specialized group, and Spark was born. Its mandate is wide but clear: 'To increase the quantity and quality of idea generation, set-up and run a process to test the commercial feasibility of ideas, and generate new breakthrough ventures which take Powergen capabilities to new markets.' The aim was to 'reuse and extend existing assets, processes, intellectual property and technology'.

After 15 months, Spark has two ventures looking for investment and has put 20 ventures through its first stage and five its second, for a total programme cost of under £5 million.

The more stages there are, the more reviews take place and the greater the number of opportunities to kill bad ventures. Stuart Degg of Royal & SunAlliance found that, 'The Financial Director liked the answer "no" to be delivered quicker. We offered a more effective way of killing ideas.'

A separate unit to buffer the activity from the mainstream

Management consultancy Booz Allen recently researched business creation in a sample of 23 international businesses. It found that 74 per cent established a separate subsidiary or division for their new venture efforts, while only 17 per cent embedded this capability within an existing business unit or division. The remaining 9 per cent created a hybrid combining in-house capabilities with a separate subsidiary or division. According to an executive, Shell found that early-stage ideas tend to be crushed by product and process improvements with better short-term payoffs. As a result, both the company-wide Gamechanger programme and its E-Initiatives unit have been run separately from its divisions.

The venture selection process channels funds to ventures, and the venture unit mediates by negotiating budgets with venture teams and providing help either directly or by corralling other resources from within the company. The venture unit and the formal staged system together provide the separation necessary for venture teams to act freely and the assurance that individuals within the teams are secure in their positions. The unit increases trust by looking after the interests of venture team staff.

Flexibility

When assembling an overall architecture, executives find that flexibility and scalability are two important properties, for several reasons. Firstly, opportunities arrive at their own rate, influenced by factors outside the company such as the economy and the rate of technology change within its industry, and the system must be able to expand and contract with the inflow of suitable opportunities. Secondly, opportunities come in all shapes and sizes. For example, Powergen's two best-developed ventures are a tiny business that sells advertising space on the sides of electricity substations and a much larger proposition ('Hole World') that plans to increase the efficiency of utility street works through a new IT planning and scheduling infrastructure. Lastly, ventures are unpredictable and can enter the system in any shape – mostly finished or completely undeveloped.

A venturing executive at ExxonMobil says, 'The process has to be flexible, as the route to innovation is never linear. Any process has to be always under development and has to incorporate the ability to insert iterative loops.' However, Beverly Bittner, Director of Strategic Business Development at Sainsbury's, warns that 'process helps you avoid the big mistakes. But too much and you don't do anything. I see process as the means to an end rather than an end in itself.'

THE BUSINESS CREATION ARCHITECTURE

The second part of this chapter builds up the elements of the business creation system and how money, people and ideas come together within it, overseen by the guiding hand of the venture unit or its equivalent. This architecture is effectively the managed market in assets, ideas, people and money that we discussed in Chapter 2, and forms the roadmap for the next six chapters of the book. Figure 5.1 (given later in this chapter) provides an overview.

Core activities

The core of the architecture is a staged venture development process by which ideas are turned into a business unit ready for major investment (which we define as 'sufficient finance to fund the business to cash flow positive'). An idea can be the barest notion of a product with no mention of customers and operational delivery. According to Tim Forrest, the goal is to develop ideas to the point where management can just 'add money and go'.

The process consists of four major activities, which we have labelled Sense, Start, Seed and Set-up. In our experience, most companies develop over time a similar model, although they use their own names for the different activities. Powergen's Spark venture unit provides us with Example 5.3.

Example 5.3   Powergen (2)

According to the picture on the wall, the Spark process takes ideas all the way to free-standing business units. Ventures start out in 'Proposition Development', where small sums are spent on desk research to establish the scale of the business opportunity and the competitive situation. Should the venture then pass the first selection hurdle, the 'Proof of Concept' stage starts. This subjects the idea to a battery of market research tests about the customer proposition, the business model and pricing.

Success in the second round of selection puts the venture through to the third and final stage – Venture Plan – where the venture team produces a full business plan to exploit the market opportunity identified in the previous stage, and a customer contract ready to sign. After this stage, the venture emerges from Spark and is evaluated by an Investment Board comprising senior Powergen executives and two external directors with venture capital experience. If approved, it tries to raise investment finance from outside to supplement agreed Powergen funding.

When, and if, this is done, a Spark Board is formed to oversee the venture. Although Spark has completed the business development job, it has two executives on the board alongside three senior managers. The latter make the difficult decisions and the Spark executives provide detailed insights on the venture to them.

Forrest maintains that Spark's use of this staged process has substantial benefits. 'We go from claim to proof to plan in the three stages. This increases the rigour behind the investment decisions we are making. We work out the touch-points and ask a standard set of questions to help us find and eliminate weaknesses. After that, we challenge the venture team to come back and show results. For instance, produce a letter of intent from a customer. This keeps costs down and maintains a delivery focus.' Also, as Forrest doesn't say, it helps the company get rid of weaker ventures before they drain the bank.

Some other companies, such as Roche Diagnostics, have a preceding stage which involves generating and regulating the flow of ideas into the system. We cover this in Chapter 8. Some, such as Diageo include one additional stage, typically by breaking

'Seed' into two because it involves two relatively expensive elements (market research and prototyping). In the end, it is easier to add a stage than to drop one, and a company can always divide Seed in two for any given venture. If there is a great deal of uncertainty about the viability of the venture or it is very expensive, then such a division can help. The stages are, in order:

- *Sense*. The inputs for the business creation system are raw ideas. They can come from staff, management, R & D technicians, and from outside the firm from sources such as consultants and bankers. The function of this first activity is to generate and regulate the flow of all such ideas into the system. This involves marketing to would-be entrepreneurs and helping them to create, express and evolve their ideas.

- *Start*. This is the low-cost development of a concept via thinking, planning, desk research and design. Its outputs are early business and financial plans with definitions of the outline customer proposition and product concept and indicative revenues and costs. It also includes the preparation of a venture team for the Seed stage.

- *Seed*. This is the major development of proposition to the point of investment decision. It involves significant amounts of 'seed' money. To move from Seed to Set-up, the venture produces market research and sales contracts to prove customers and revenues, and through prototyping and supply contracts proves product logistics and costs. It also requires complete business and financial plans.

- *Set-up*. This is the formal establishment of a business unit once investment is agreed. It includes the formation of the business, transfer of staff, hiring of management and appointment of non-executives, setting of targets and incentives, remuneration, and decisions on links with the parent company.

This sequence of activities can be viewed in two ways. One is as a filtering process. At each stage, a small number of ideas or projects are selected to move forward, and the rest are stopped. In this regard it is not unlike the graduate recruitment process for a big multinational company, where 10 000 applications yields 1000 on-campus interviews, 200 second-round interviews, 40 job offers and 20 acceptances.

However, the sequence of activities is also a development process, in which value is added at each stage. The raw idea is worked up into a concrete proposal, a team of people is put together, market

Table 5.1 Final outputs from the four-stage process

Item	Description	Function
Business plan	Description of the opportunity and strategy to exploit it, the competition, and of the business model, products, marketing, operations and staff	Persuasion
Financial plan	Revenues and costs details. Calculation of NPV and IRR	Persuasion
Prototype	Demonstrator for market research and costs planning	Evidence
Market research	Evidence of customer numbers and revenues per customer to support financial plan and assist product design	Evidence
Supply contracts	Outline contracts for supply of critical product components	Evidence
Sales contracts	Outline contracts to purchase products	Evidence
Venture team	Nucleus of future business unit. Multidisciplinary	Readiness
Venture setup	Goal-setting, non-executive management, positioning of venture and its relationship with firm	Readiness
Venture management	Management team for future business unit	Readiness

research is done, and so forth. Viewed in this way, the process is really about generating the necessary set of outputs that are required before investment can be sought. Table 5.1 summarizes the final set of outputs that are typically needed, divided by purpose – persuasion, evidence or readiness.

The plans persuade investors to invest. A prototype, market research and supply and sales contracts together back up the claims and promises made in the plans, while the hiring of the venture's management and staff, and other Set-up work, get the venture ready to operate. Venture teams produce these outputs in a certain order, determined by a cheapest-first uncertainty-reducing logic that we elaborate in Chapter 6.

Selection process

The four core activities are overlaid by two more. The first is a *selection* process, which operates continuously. The underlying purpose of selection is to reduce wastage by eliminating ventures as soon as a fatal weakness appears and to reapply resources to stronger ventures. The earlier a fatal flaw is discovered in a business proposition the more resources are saved in not prototyping, not doing expensive market research and not writing a business plan. The importance of selection cannot be overstated; in fact, the art of business creation largely consists of killing poor ventures as soon as possible.

The venture unit, which knows most about the venture, plays an equally significant role and at Powergen and Diageo selection is done exclusively by the venture unit in the early stages of development. At later stages and for larger sums, venture teams may go before an investment board (called 'venture review board' in this book), composed of senior management, which reviews their plans and decides whether to fund the next stage. The selection vehicle, like the entire system, must be neutral and transparent. It remains so by using criteria and by the publication of assessments against each criterion.

Support activities

The second overlay is a set of support activities that are provided to the individuals and teams who are working on each individual venture. Almost always in *Focused* companies, these support activities are carried out by a venture unit, though occasionally a business development or strategic planning group provides some of them. For the purposes of this discussion, and for the subsequent chapters, we assume that a venture unit provides support.

This venture unit does more than its nearest equivalent in the open market, the business angel. Overall, it combines the functions of professor, doctor and engineer. As professors, the unit's staff teach venture teams and coach them through the complexities of the venture development process. As doctors, they diagnose problems and help teams solve them. Finally, as engineers, they get their hands dirty by working on venture development themselves. For management, the venture unit keeps costs low and buffers ventures from operating units.

Money

Money oils the wheels of business creation. The venture unit has prime responsibility for identifying and accessing sources of funds for new ventures and managing budgets. As we have already espoused, business creation is a low-cost approach to business development.

Management and protection

Rick Wills of British Airways sums up the role nicely. 'We arbitrated between intrapreneurs and the company.' Acting as doctor and engineer, the unit is a buffer between management and the venture team, providing separation for both sides, security to the entrepreneur and simplification for management.

Assistance and advice

The venture unit acts as professor and engineer here. Its members may work in the venture team for short periods while staff are recruited, and the unit provides guidance on the wide array of business issues that a venture has to deal with, and scours the company and the outside world for specialist help.

Powergen's Spark unit always seconds one person to each venture and provides venture teams access to its finance, retail, technology and business skills. Tim Forrest says, 'We try to fit the Spark person in to rectify weaknesses in the venture team, and we take great care to match working styles too. But, more importantly, we have found that the Spark person forces a delivery focus. Many venture teams, particularly at the beginning, need this. Different people are involved at different stages in ventures and not every activity in the process needs a full-time person for the full period.'

Strategy and business development

The venture unit has the additional role of linking its business creation efforts to the broader strategic priorities of the company. To do that, it has to sit close to the strategy function and the rest of business development. For example, the Director of Ericsson Business Innovation reports to the board, which includes the CEO, the Finance Director, the head of Strategic Marketing and the CTO. At Lloyds TSB the head of its Strategic Ventures unit reports to the Group Strategy Director, while the head of the company's acquisitions function, the Group Corporate Development Director, sits on the Strategic Ventures investment committee.

Charting the entire system

Figure 5.1 provides an overview of the business creation architecture, derived from those we have investigated at Powergen, Roche, Lloyds TSB, Unilever, Schlumberger, British Airways, Diageo, BAT, Siemens, Panasonic, Nokia, Shell, and BT.

There are three core venture development activities – Start, Seed and Set-up. These are preceded by the idea gathering activity – Sense – and overlaid by the selection process and the support

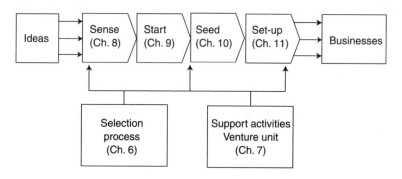

Figure 5.1 Business creation architecture

activities. Together, these turn money, people and ideas into businesses ready to receive major investment.

This figure provides a roadmap for the next seven chapters. We describe the selection process next (Chapter 6), because it is used in all the core activities, and then we follow it with a look at the characteristics and role of the venture unit or its equivalent (Chapter 7). The venture development process is described in Chapters 8–11 (one activity per chapter), while Chapter 12 is the final chapter in this section, looking at venturing from the perspective of the corporate entrepreneur.

COSTS

We have outlined a system by which ventures can be started, selected and developed and said that it helps reduce costs and risks firstly by killing ventures quickly and secondly by making development more orderly and efficient. How much, in practice does venturing cost a firm?

Business creation costs divide into two parts: venture development (including the costs of operating the venture unit, if there is one) and venture investment. Investment decisions involve top executives and are a facet of strategic management, and we cover them in Chapter 14. The key point to understand is that development spending generates well-researched ventures, complete with plans and teams, which fit with the company's strategy and business assets.

Venture costs

The cost of an individual venture (i.e. turning an idea into an investment-ready business) is driven by its scale and its familiarity according to Fig. 2.3 (our Business Development Model). The less familiar it is, the more the firm has to create new assets to execute it. At some point on Fig. 2.3, as scale rises and familiarity falls, the firm looks for a joint venture partner to provide useful assets and to defray financial risk. After all, why go to the expense of creating new assets – a new brand, new customer channels, a new technology – if somebody else will let you have access to theirs?

The bare minimum effort required to develop a venture is three staff for about four months to do some market research, write the plans and carry out some product and technology due diligence. This comes in at about $300 000, including salaries. A billion dollar opportunity is likely to take a larger team a year to develop properly, involve in-depth qualitative and quantitative market research in several countries and require substantial product development and perhaps legal work, the use of external consultants and experts and considerable management time. This is unlikely to cost less than $10 million.

At Lucent New Ventures Group, the average Seed cost was $1 million, and at BG Group (part of the former UK utility British Gas) it was around $500 000 for small ventures in the $25 million to 50 million revenue opportunity range. Our research suggests a cost range of between 1 and 3 per cent of the revenue opportunity. Larger ventures tend to sit at the lower end and unfamiliar ventures at the upper end. Of this sum, around 80 per cent is spent in the Seed stage and 20 per cent in the Start stage. The principal costs in venture development are market research, staff and product development, and in Chapters 9 and 10 we show how to keep these costs down by deferring the more expensive activities, especially product development, until they are strictly necessary.

Venturing costs

Most of the companies we have spoken to spend between $3 million and $10 million per year on the venture development part of business creation. This buys somewhere between two and 10 investment opportunities, depending on their scale and familiarity. A former executive in BG Group's venture unit puts the minimum venture unit budget at $3 million. Below this level the unit cannot produce more than four average ($500 000 development cost) investment opportunities per year which, says the executive, is the minimum sustainable size for a business creation capability. We conclude for calibration purposes that a venturing spend of $5 million buys the option to invest in annual revenue opportunities of between $160 million and $500 million.

CONCLUSION

In this chapter we have made six major points about the business creation architecture:

■ Venturing is a creative, risky and complex investment activity which is fundamentally different from day-to-day divisional operations.

■ A *Focused* firm needs processes and tools with which to manage business creation. These have to satisfy management needs (risk and cost control, no disruption) and entrepreneur needs (freedom, resources and help, security) while taking account of business creation's characteristics.

■ These processes and tools must incorporate various elements – selection and planning, staged development, separation from operations, and flexibility.

■ A four-part development process (Sense, Start, Seed, Set-up) turns ideas into businesses ready for investment. A formal selection process kills poor ventures quickly.

■ A venture unit provides the security, help and freedom that entrepreneurs want while acting as a disciplined capability hub for management in the early stages of venturing.

■ Each dollar of venture development spending generates the option to invest in annual revenue opportunity 30–100 times greater. A reasonable minimum annual spend to sustain the capability for a Fortune 500 firm is $3 million.

6 Selecting Ventures

In the last chapter we said that the essence of venturing is selecting the good and killing the bad, so that resources are applied to projects with high revenue potential and strategic fit rather than (as was the case with Kudu in Chapter 1) to the first ideas that come along. Equally, nothing alienates the broad mass of managers in the operating divisions of a firm, and the CFO, more than a venture unit wasting P & L money on a ragbag of semi-relevant ventures that are not really going anywhere. Any firm that gets selection right is half-way to developing its business creation capability and cementing it into its everyday activities.

Selection, then, has to be tough and continuous. Many people use the metaphor of a funnel to explain this selection process. The idea is that a rapidly-narrowing funnel collects a broad set of ideas, and then this set is rapidly narrowed and filtered until a select few emerge at the other end. This metaphor is clearly right – all good selection systems work this way. However, it only partly explains how business creation selection is done in practice. As ventures develop, selection takes place on the basis of work already done in certain areas *and* on the potential of the venture in other areas where work has yet to be done. Recall Tim Forrest's 'claim to proof to plan' description of the venture development process. Selectors first assess claims (before Start) and then begin to judge the proof of the opportunity and its relevance to the firm (before Seed). Before investment (Set-up), they rigorously judge both the proof of, and the plans to exploit, the opportunity.

Selection is, therefore, intertwined with the venture development process. We, like executives at Powergen and Roche, see venture development as similar to a university PhD. Consider the analogy: a typical PhD programme involves 2 years of training in research methods followed by 2 years of research culminating in a dissertation and a rigorous grilling by professors. A professor guides the students throughout, setting the agenda, asking questions, monitoring the students' work and coaching them through to the award of the gown.

Venture development is indeed similar. The venture team is the student, the venture unit the professor (and doctor and engineer), and the venture review board members (and ultimately the investors) play the role of the grilling professors. In this view, the business opportunity is the thesis and the business plan is the dissertation – a set of demonstrably true statements that cover the subject exhaustively, prove the thesis, and leave no relevant questions unanswered. Both processes are concerned with using empirical techniques to produce information that reduces uncertainty to a sufficiently low level for the purpose of PhD award, in the case of a university, or investment funding, in the case of a business.

The information theorist Claude Shannon (1916–2001) summed this up in six words: 'Information is the reduction of uncertainty.' We can derive a vital lesson for the venture development process, and hence the way selection works, from this analysis:

> Carry out venture development activities in descending order of uncertainty-reducing 'bang for buck' to the point where venture uncertainty is low enough for investment.

This has powerful and desirable risk- and cost-reducing results for the firm involved in business creation. At one extreme, if there is no uncertainty about the venture, forget venture development and get on with building and selling product. At the other, if it would cost too much to reduce uncertainty to an acceptable level, forget the venture and fund something else. For ventures at neither extreme, this approach governs the order in which activities are carried out, so that ventures with a fatal flaw are killed as cheaply as possible. For example, there is no point in carrying out product development in a pre-investment venture if there is little doubt about product design and feasibility. Resources are better spent in areas where there is greater uncertainty and where the killer question may lurk.

HOW TO SELECT

Selection is ideally made on the basis of a transparent and methodical system, but this is often not realized. Consider the example of a new venture by Portisco, a European telecommunications equipment firm (Example 6.1). Here, selection was carried out informally by a single senior executive at the beginning of the venture.

Example 6.1   Portisco's ill-conceived joint venture

In June 2001, Portisco's Managed Services division set up a joint venture named Accordant with a UK drug discovery firm, BioScientific, as part of its strategy to move up the value chain from equipment to managed services, applications and content. The press release stated that Accordant was 'to integrate and leverage Portisco's broad-band data transmission and hosting capabilities with Bioscientific's proteome databases and its data analysis software tools'. Accordant was a 50:50 joint venture.

According to an executive on the Portisco venture team, Nabil Malik, the business was conceived by Finance Director Naomi Morris and passed to a Managed Services executive. Morris deemed a medical opportunity to be relevant because Portisco had a medical diagnostic imaging group and because access to large medical databases requires high bandwidth.

According to Malik, the deal was opportunistic and the team was under pressure from Morris to meet a deadline. The atmosphere was 'quick, aggressive, do deals'. Although market research was done and a business plan produced, the review process 'was probably not rigorous enough'. Furthermore, the finance staff who were responsible for that review worked in Morris' department. 'You have an understanding of limits,' says Malik diplomatically. 'The grilling did happen. But you bring a finance person on board and get there judiciously.'

Portisco later found that its attempt to create telecommunications demand via Accordant was a step too far up the value chain. Accordant was supposed to buy managed services from Portisco, but the latter subsequently withdrew from this market and Accordant went elsewhere.

The lack of a formal process and one-off single-person selection caused a dubious deal-led venture to get the go-ahead at Portisco. This method is haphazard because in business, as in life, the answer you get depends on whom you ask. However, in business creation, the answer you get cannot depend on whom you ask. Arms-length procedures are vital, because without them bad projects, inconsistency, controversy and a rapid flight back to *Ad Hoc* are all on the cards. Roche Diagnostics, a division of Basle-based Roche, uses a more formal method, (Example 6.2).

Example 6.2   Roche Diagnostics' selection process

Roche Diagnostics puts ventures through several stages before they look for major investment. For Stage 2 projects, the team requests further funding at the regular meeting of the divisional executive committee, which acts as the venture review board. For Stage 3 projects, which have more developed business plans ready for further investment, the review board is smaller and more focused. Before each formal evaluation comes the 'grilling' which, says venture unit manager Lonnie Shoff, 'is like an academic review'. These grilling sessions help venture teams strengthen their proposal before the formal evaluation. Because several of the grillers are also on the board, it provides each side with a good inkling of what to expect from

the other. The method has been so successful that the divisional CTO
is using it to assess R & D projects.

Both Stage 2 and 3 projects are evaluated using a set of criteria.
These include, in no particular order, relevance to Roche Diagnostics'
assets, the size of the revenue opportunity, the team, sustainable
competitive advantage (usually meaning the level of proprietary IPR
that the venture expects to create) and a risk management plan.
Roche Diagnostics is working to make the selection process more
transparent by further developing these criteria and the way they are
used. One benefit of using criteria, says Shoff, is communications.
There have been occasions when venture teams who are unclear
about the process have phoned up the Divisional CEO.

Roche Diagnostics uses formal criteria throughout venture
development, and selection is carried by a venture review board
made up of divisional management with the power and resources
to steer ventures through to the end (Example 6.2). This
combination of criteria and senior executive review board has
several advantages:

■   *Control.* Management can ensure the fit of ventures with
     strategy and company assets and adjust the scale of business
     creation activity to the financial position of the firm and the
     level of opportunities flowing into it.

■   *Transparency.* Management, staff and outsiders can see how
     and why projects are selected, increasing the accountability of
     the venture unit and the level of trust in the system. Venture
     teams can see that the unit is making decisions fairly, system-
     atically and without bias while management can see that the
     venture unit is being responsible when selecting and
     developing early-stage ventures. The venture unit can also
     communicate its selection methods and more legitimately
     refuse to sponsor projects.

■   *Comparability.* Management can ensure consistency of
     selection across ideas, time and individual selectors.

- *Risk and cost reduction.* Too many bad projects continue because those in control cannot articulate why the project deserves to be terminated. With formal criteria, the venture unit can more easily remove projects.

The need for consistency across time and ideas suggests that the venture unit and venture review board use the same set of criteria throughout the venture development process. Tim Forrest at Powergen attests, 'In selection we use the same tests all the way along. We demand a higher degree of quality of answer as time goes on. This maintains the rigour behind the decisions we are making.'

The more senior the board the better. The Spark group at Powergen uses a venture panel for Seed-stage ventures. It typically includes a managing director of a business unit, a financial director, a lawyer, two non-executives from outside the company, one venture capitalist and an incubation expert. Vince Forlenza, SVP and head of venturing at Becton Dickinson, operates a strong review board that includes the CEO, the CFO, the heads of the three major business units, the general counsel and the Corporate Medical Director.

From these examples we can see that the venture review board has other responsibilities than just selection. The board also:

- Assists venture with operational and strategy questions.

- Monitors the performance of the venture unit and its management.

- Sponsors venture teams, opens doors and deals with reluctant middle managers.

- Promotes business creation, the venture unit and its ventures.

These areas will be addressed in subsequent chapters.

SELECTION CRITERIA

We have developed a set of selection criteria from our research that are communicable, unambiguous and helpful to both management and venture team. We have divided them into six categories: strategic, product, marketing, organizational, financial and risk. These categories are the section headings of a good business plan, and underneath them sit the questions that a venture team has to answer to get investment funding.

Applying the criteria: a worked example

These selection criteria can best be illustrated through Example 6.3: the case of the Millennium Experience in London. We reckon that had the UK Government considered the venture at the outset using these six criteria it could have uncovered six potential problems. The example also illustrates how the decisions made at the beginning of the venture can govern what unfolds as it develops, and hence the role of the venture review board.

Example 6.3   The Millennium Experience

The Millennium Experience, held in London's Millennium Dome during the year 2000, was a government venture that went right and wrong. The latest of a series of three vast exhibitions in London since 1850, it opened at midnight on 31 December 1999 with a gala gathering of the great and good, and closed on plan exactly a year later. In that year, the Experience became one of the most successful start-up visitor attractions in history, generating over £90 million in revenues from 6.5 million visitors, most of them transported to the elegant venue in south-east London in gleaming trains on a new showcase 'Tube' line. Visitor satisfaction ratings were in the mid-eighties per cent, and many made repeat visits.

Despite this success, the Experience damaged the reputation for competent management that the Blair government had acquired in its first 4 years in office. The budget was £750 million, of which £170 million was to come from revenues and the rest from the National Lottery and sponsorships. However, revenues came in 40 per cent under and, as 2000 progressed, the event had to be bailed out repeatedly.

Strategic

This category questions the relevance of the idea to the company – which assets it will use and extend, and whether the idea fits with the company's business strategy – and helps determine whether business creation (as opposed to acquisition or venture capital) is the right approach to the opportunity in the first place. It also questions whether the idea has potential for initial competitive advantage through access to those assets and sustainable competitive advantage through lock-in, high switching costs, and so on.

Although it owned the land, the UK Government had no competence in designing, developing or operating visitor attractions such as the Millennium Experience, nor did it have any assets that could benefit from the experience it would gain. Our Business Development Model (Fig. 2.3) suggests that, because of the unfamiliarity and scale of the venture, the government should have either injected the land and the building into a joint venture with, or created and sold a licence to, an attraction operator such as Disney. Instead, the UK Government chose to retain total control and formed a subsidiary company. This was the first problem.

Product and operations

Once the venture review board is satisfied that the project passes muster strategically, it reviews whether the product concept is valid and credible, whether the technology and processes to build the product are tenable and whether the customer's usage of the product can be supported and maintained.

The Millennium Experience project was feasible from a product, operations and technology point of view. But two factors needed particular attention. The second problem was the transport of visitors to the remote site in East London. The Experience depended on the completion of London Underground's extension of the Jubilee Line and its new station next to the Millennium Dome, although at the time the go-ahead was given to the Experience, the completion of the line was still on target for a 1998 opening. The third problem was a deadline that could only be shifted if the UK moved off the Julian calendar.

Marketing

The customer proposition, which we define as 'how the product supports which activities by what types of customers', is the key part of this important criterion. After this comes the method of revenue generation and collection (the revenue model), the state of the industry and competitive factors, and questions about marketing channels, promotion and branding.

The Millennium Experience venture was unlikely to, and never did, have any problems with proposition (a day out for all the family), differentiation (unique), channels (tickets on sale by Internet, telephone and through newsagents), branding (The Millennium) or promotion (advertising and combo deals). Inside a world-class piece of architecture designed by Richard Rogers of Lloyds of London and Centre Georges Pompidou fame, the Experience was a marvellous marketing proposition. The 12 million visitors forecast in the budget implied that the Experience would set new records for the first year of a visitor attraction. This was the fourth major problem.

Organization

This criterion covers the venture team and is composed of team completeness, capabilities, dedication and motivation. At the Dome, the original management team consisted mostly of career civil servants with little knowledge of building and operating events on such a large scale. This was the fifth major problem.

Financial

This criterion covers the scale of the revenue opportunity and its attractiveness in terms of profit and margin potential, Net Present

Value (NPV) and Internal Rate of Return (IRR). Companies need to understand what may drive revenues down and costs up so that they can assess the sensitivity of NPV and IRR to changes in assumptions.

The main drivers for the Millennium Experience were visitor numbers (revenues) and exhibition design and construction (costs), but insufficient financial contingency appears to have been built in to the original budget. According to one Experience executive, 'there was no Plan B'. This was the sixth major problem.

Risks

Each of the five categories has risks. This criterion evaluates the nature and level of risk in each of these, how well the venture team has analysed them, and the extent to which it has contingency plans to mitigate any adverse outcomes. The Millennium Experience venture was loaded down with six unsolved problems at the beginning. Two of these were product and operations, one marketing, one organizational, one financial and one strategic. Collectively, these represented a grave risk to the venture.

In the event, the Experience opened on time after rapid construction of the building and its contents, although a problem with security scanners on the opening night stranded many of the world's newspaper and magazine editors on a cold platform far from the Dome and publicity on 2 January 2000 was disastrous. 'Only' 6.5 million of the expected 12 million visitors showed up, necessitating repeated bailouts and the replacement of the management team halfway through 2000.

The 1-year duration of the show was the greatest single error. Original market research showed that the overall potential market was around a third of the 60 million population of the UK and its 30 million annual visitors. The Millennium Experience could have expected 6–8 million visitors and £100–150 million revenues per year in perpetuity.

This is the kind of thing that goes on in highly politicized environments, and corporations are by no means immune from such pressures. Our view, though, is that a corporate venture review board using formal criteria could, at the point of the investment decision, have worked its way through to the right six questions and exposed the problems.

THE SELECTION AND DEVELOPMENT PROCESS

As development proceeds, the venture unit and the review board look at a combination of the answers ('proofs') to outstanding questions and hypotheses ('claims') about the next batch of questions. No venture team can answer all of these questions at the beginning of the process. Instead, it answers them batch by batch and builds up a case for investment so that, by the end, no unsubstantiated claims remain. For example, a venture may get through to the Start stage because its advocates airily cite a $25 million revenue opportunity. By the time the Seed stage has finished, however, the revenue opportunity has to be calculated with some precision and backed up with detailed market research.

Selection takes place continuously, with formal review points before each stage. The more rigorous and regular these checkups, the better served the venture unit and the parent company. Persistent screening enables management to monitor progress within ventures, to measure venture performance against milestones and targets, to watch for signs of trouble within the venture, to allocate rewards and incentives and ultimately to keep venture managers on the ball. Tim Forrest says, 'We use milestones set before we start each stage which tell the entrepreneurs what we want them to demonstrate. We work out the touch-points, set milestones, ask a standard set of questions. We aim to eliminate weaknesses. We then challenge the group to come back and show the results.'

The 'bang for buck' rule dictates the order of work in the venture, and we have divided our questions into three batches and matched them to the venture development stages that we outlined in Chapter 5. In general, strategy is cheap, market

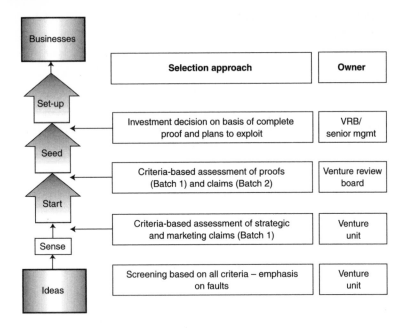

Figure 6.1 Staged venture selection

research is medium and product development is expensive. *Focused* firms mostly work in that order. Diageo's New Business Ventures group, for instance, works out the strategic fit, establishes the market and its risks and then defines the product. Roche Diagnostics establishes customer proposition, followed by the revenue opportunity via market research, and only then does some prototyping.

Figure 6.1 shows who does selection at each stage and the approach to it.

Before start

Once ideas have started to flow, venture units spend more of their time screening ideas (getting rid of rubbish) than selecting them (picking the excellent). The screening process looks at the project's potential and the claims of the venture's proponents, especially those relating to scale, customer need and relevance to the company. The venture unit does not always have to do the screening. At ExxonMobil, the R & D groups do it: 'They investigate everything that seems possible and impossible and establish feasibility. Then screening comes in as a way of identifying which of the feasible ideas should be investigated. Only once a large number of ideas have been investigated is a process of selection then applied', says one venture executive.

We recommend a 2-week investigation, during which the venture team has to develop credible answers for six Batch 1 marketing and strategy questions:

- Is the product concept coherent?

- Is the customer proposition coherent?

- What is the revenue opportunity?

- What company assets does it propose to use?

- What assets does this business need to succeed?

- Does this idea fit with the company's current strategy?

We define 'product concept' and its counterpart 'customer proposition' more fully in Chapter 8. These are the fundamental building blocks of any new venture, and relate to each other closely. A well-worked customer proposition expressed solely in terms of the customer, without mentioning the venture or the parent firm at all, is the principal cure for 'subject think', and without it there is no venture. The 'scale' question helps to eliminate small and irrelevant ventures. The two 'assets' strategy questions take us back again to Fig. 2.3, and help eliminate ideas which are better suited to another business development technique or which are too far away from the company's core business. The 'fit' question helps ensure coherence between business development and strategy.

During the 2-week Sense investigation stage, the team has to make reasonable claims in each of these six areas so that the selectors can assess them. We have seen a number of different models for evaluating and selecting early-stage ideas. Nokia's

New Growth Business unit has two staff undertaking early selection. One of them, Johan Schmid, reports that, 'We believe in acting fast and acting on experience as much as anything else. Business units have their own clear perspective, so we listen to them, but do not necessarily act on their advice. We can go against the tide, but ultimately we want their buy in.' This illustrates, incidentally, that the number of people making decisions is less important than that the right people make them. At Powergen, the Spark venture unit uses a larger panel to review young projects. The panel consists of one venture 'sponsor', who promotes the venture, and three 'neutrals', who make the decision. Members of the venture unit fill the neutral positions by rotation.

Before Seed

During the Start stage, the team's job is to provide a proof of the six claims made in Sense and also to work-up some new claims (see Batch 2, below) for evaluation by the venture review board. The decision to proceed to the Seed stage depends on the quality of proofs and the credibility of the Batch 2 claims.

The key claim questions for the venture team during the Start stage are in Batch 2, and include questions in the marketing and organizational (team) categories, with a smattering of product questions:

- What is the revenue model?

- What is the customer segmentation?

- What is the pricing?

- How are products like this differentiated from each other? Where does this product fit in?

- What is the intensity of competition in this product category?

- How will the product be sold? What channels are necessary?

- How will it be branded and promoted?

- Does the product technology work?

- Can the product actually be produced and operated?

- Does the team have sufficient skills?

- Is there a complete team to develop this business? If not, can one be recruited?

- What is the team's level of motivation and dedication?

The first six of these points are all concerned with marketing viability, and more specifically about the ability of the team to differentiate the new product offering from those of competitors. The questions about channels and promotion are necessary to show that the team knows how to deliver to customers and attract their attention. Equally, teams have to be sure about how technology affects their proposition, and be able to assure reviewers that it performs as needed. Finally, there are the obligatory questions about the venture team. It is well known that venture capitalists always ask about the team, and business creation review boards are no different.

The decision to enter the Seed stage is made by the venture review board. We have already shown that the more senior the board's members, the better. The venture review boards need a process to:

- Scrutinize each venture from all points of view.

- Provide a mechanism for achieving consensus.

- Structure discussion about the venture.

- Provide a means to communicate feedback to the venture team.

We recommend that venture review boards structure their meetings around these questions and use a simple scoring system. This focuses discussion on disagreements between individuals, illustrates where a venture is strong and weak, and allows a group to work its way towards consensus. As stated in Chapter 4 when discussing how to use our business creation audit, executives should not average their scores to generate a group view as this drives evaluations towards the middle of the range and group-think prevails. Instead, they should attempt to come to a consensus view in each category.

Before Set-up

To enter the Set-up stage, the venture team has to convince top management with work done in the Seed stage that its proposed business is worthy of full-scale investment. While the venture unit and the venture review board have a part to play at this stage, the decision to commit resources is almost always taken at the top of the company.

Other than the involvement of top management, there are two major differences between Set-up and Seed decisions. Firstly, some firms require corroboration from either a business division or an external party such as a venture capital firm. Powergen usually insists that new ventures gain external financial support, Ericsson needs to have the support of another internal business unit, while Becton Dickinson insists on the agreement of its venture capital unit. Secondly, the investment decision is made on the basis of all the questions listed so far, plus those following. During Seed all claims are replaced by proofs.

This last set, Batch 3, focuses on remaining strategic, financial and risk questions, answers to which can only be produced at the end of the process once everything else has been worked out. Batch 3 also looks at more difficult product questions, work on which is usually not necessary before Seed:

- What initial advantages does this business have over its competitors?

- What sustainable advantages will it create – barriers to entry, stickiness, switching costs, etc?

- Will the business create a new asset or extend an existing one?

- Can the product's use by customers be supported?

- Can the product be maintained?

- Is the opportunity financially attractive? What is its NPV for a range of sensible discount rates? What is its IRR?

- What are the main cost and revenue drivers?

- What are the main marketing and product risks? What pre-emptive measures are in place?

- What are the main organizational risks? What pre-emptive measures are in place?

- What are the main strategic risks? What pre-emptive measures are in place?

- What are the financial risks? Are the NPV and IRR robust? What happens to them if the values of the cost and revenue drivers are adjusted?

A venture executive at BG Group couched the initial advantage question as, 'What competitive advantage using the firm's assets – geographical reach, technology and energy distribution experience – do you get?' There is no point in a firm proceeding with a venture unless it provides a strong competitive advantage. If it does not, but the opportunity is still financially attractive, then immediate spinning-out is probably the best option.

The two product questions look at how the venture team plans to manage the logistics of inputs to and outputs from the product. Ventures often underestimate the scale of infrastructure that is necessary to deliver a product to its customers.

Many companies create NPV or IRR hurdles, although fixing these only encourages ventures to exaggerate. Few companies do proper financial risk analysis of new ventures, which entails knowledge of revenue and cost drivers.

Risk questions allow management to remove ventures which appear flawed. The best approach is to quantify risks through the financial plan. Clearly, organizational and more qualitative marketing, product and strategic risks have to be subject to judgment as well as numerical analysis, but the 'bottom line' always has to be exactly that – the bottom line – rather than subjective assertions. Venture teams, for their part, benefit by being compelled to consider everything that could go wrong with their venture and to plan remedies in advance.

If all product, marketing, organization and related risk questions have been satisfactorily answered during the venture development process, then top management can stress the two high-level categories – strategic and financial. We cover these last two categories, and the investment decision, in Chapter 11.

CONCLUSION

In this chapter we have made seven major points about venture selection and the venture development process:

■ The purpose of venture development is to reduce uncertainty to the point where investment is possible.

■ The venture development process and selection are intertwined. Venture teams develop proofs and claims in each of the 'S' stages so that ventures can be evaluated for entry into the next stage. For investment (entry into Set-up), all claims are proven.

■ The use of formal criteria provides various benefits, among them control, transparency, comparability and risk and cost reduction.

■ Six criteria categories – strategic, product and operations, marketing, organizational, financial and risks – between them cover all the questions that need to be asked about a venture.

■ Because of their relative costs, strategy comes first, marketing second and product development third during venture development. The selection process follows.

■ A venture review board staffed by senior management with sufficient authority should select ventures for Seed investment. This board also assists ventures and sponsors business creation.

■   Continuous selection by the venture unit, and formal staged selection by the unit and the venture review board, enables better venture management and the use of targets and deadlines.

7 The Venture Unit

Professional coaches in team sports have an unenviable job. On one side is the management and its commercial concerns. Then there are the fans, each with their own heartfelt opinions about who should be playing and in what position and with an absurdly detailed memory of *that game* in 1981. On the other side are the players, most of them better paid than the coach, some with a personal brand and newspaper coverage, one or two as temperamental as racehorses. How does the coach juggle all these contrasting needs and styles? By keeping them apart, focusing on the matter at hand, and with consummate diplomacy.

We have discussed how a venture unit plays an important role in establishing a firm's business creation capability. We showed that it looks after its two customers – management and venture teams – and provides each what it needs while managing the creativity, uncertainty and complexity of the venture development process. This is not quite as hard as the sports coach's job. The venture unit manager and the venture teams have no fans – whether this is good or bad we cannot say. In contrast, though, the venture unit usually has to start business creation from nothing. At the top of the venture unit is the person with the toughest job of all: moving the firm from *Ad Hoc* to *Focused* with the minimum number of failed ventures and at minimum cost in a resource-constrained and possibly political environment.

This chapter complements sections in each of the venture development process chapters (Chapters 9, 10 and 11), where we describe the assistance and help that the unit provides to venture teams, and in Chapter 8, where we describe how the venture unit generates and attracts new business ideas. In this chapter we concentrate on how to construct the venture unit, what kind of people work in it and how it operates.

VENTURE UNIT LIFECYCLE

At Roche Diagnostics, a specialized unit drives business creation across the division. The overall goal of CEO Heino von Prondzynski, however, is to embed venturing throughout his division, which is likely to mean a steady decentralization of the activity. In fact, in the more entrepreneurial parts of the division such as its US affiliate, this has already happened. We argued earlier that venture units are a necessary part of the evolution of a company's business creation activities from *Ad Hoc* through *Focused* and on to *Integrated*, and von Prondzynski is following this model closely. Figure 7.1 shows how the role of the unit mutates over time.

The dynamic runs as follows. When venturing starts, the venture unit acts as the hub for the firm's business creation capability. It

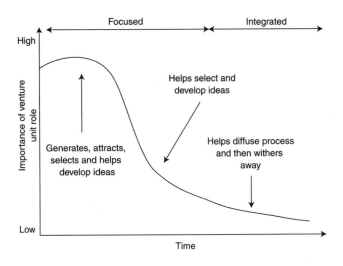

Figure 7.1 The venture unit lifecycle

focuses on generating a flow of good business opportunities and whittling them down to those worth seed capital. Venture unit staff provide the bulk of the firm's venture development expertise, and the unit spends considerable effort defining selection criteria, setting up a venture review board and putting in place the other elements of the system.

The importance of idea generation then reduces as management, staff and external people become familiar with the goals and methods of venturing. After the first few ventures have been developed, the unit concentrates on the mechanics of business development, helping teams in the way we describe in later chapters, and in the selection of young projects and the placement of invested projects.

We have observed venturing alumni at Royal & SunAlliance and BAT diffuse business creation techniques across the firm and encourage business units and divisions to set up their own processes. Once the firm has an *Integrated* approach to business creation, the original unit becomes part of the corporate business development function, working alongside strategy, acquisition and venture capital. Like Karl Marx's communist state, the venture unit withers away once its job is done.

UK retailer Sainsbury's decided in late 2001 to add a venturing support and selection function to its Strategy and Business Development group in order to provide more coherence to its business creation activities. Executives are clear, however, that they have not centralized business creation. Instead, they aim to provide many of the goodies – process, selection, support and assistance – that we define in Chapter 5 without stifling the firm's entrepreneurial spirit by creating an all-powerful central hub. According to one executive, 'Our aim is to ensure that all new start-ups are dealt with in the best possible way'. Given that many of the core business creation capabilities were present at Sainsbury's before this decision was made, the company is doing the right thing by moving from the upper reaches of the *Ad Hoc* approach and quickly through a simplified *Focused* stage and then on to *Integrated*.

There is a lesson here that we alluded to in Section 1. Venture units are more valuable when the company has few business creation capabilities. Therefore, a firm whose capabilities are well-advanced according to the business creation audit may want to take the Sainsbury's approach.

BUILDING THE VENTURE UNIT

Business creation has long-term strategic and financial goals which are hard to define and harder to measure. Venture units therefore need top management support in their early days as they walk the *Focused* tightrope. All of this fades into the background, however, once the unit starts work. The job is to select and develop ventures that fit with the firm's strategy and its strategic assets, and then to establish venturing processes and attitudes across the firm so that they become embedded.

Some venture units are created by visionary management, some under the radar by renegade managers, and others evolve from R&D groups or from corporate venture capital units keen to invest inside as well as outside. All of them face the same problems of how big a group to build, and how to staff, fund and structure the operation.

Size of group

We have encountered a wide variety of operating models. At one extreme are the teams built by Royal & SunAlliance and Shell. Royal & SunAlliance, at its peak, employed almost 40 staff in its venture unit, while Shell employed a similar number in its E-Initiatives group. At the other end of the scale is Roche, with one person. In the middle lies the bulk of firms, with somewhere between four and ten professional staff. Ericsson, for example, has eight staff, while Nokia has three people in its New Growth Business team.

We can call these two extremes 'flexible' and 'fixed'. The flexible venture unit is small and staffed by multidisciplinary people, each of whom can do any venturing job, from generating ideas, to selecting and developing them, to setting up new businesses and appointing a management team. The unit brings in staff from inside and outside the firm on a temporary basis to develop ventures, and they stay with the venture if it is invested and leave if it fails. These venture unit staff have good networks and are typically drawn from the company's top executives or potential executives. Financially, this model is low fixed-cost and high variable. The fixed venture unit, in contrast, is large and staffed with specialists split along functional lines. These units sometimes undertake venture development entirely by themselves. Financially, this model is high fixed-cost and low variable.

We favour the flexible model because the fixed model does not allow the firm to scale its activities to its level of opportunities. It is expensive, provides a target for finance during hard times and, the larger the group, the more the iron law of bureaucratic displacement bites ('in large organizations productive activity tends to be displaced by unproductive activity'). Finally, the larger the group, the more likely it is, for example, to buy its own top-of-the-line coffee machine and thereby incur the envy of line management across the firm. Truly entrepreneurial outfits, in contrast, base themselves in the coffee shop outside the head office.

Of course, these models are caricatures. At Lloyds TSB Michael Pearson has a team of nine staff, of whom six work on specific ventures, one on idea generation and the remaining two on screening, selection and initial investigation. Lloyds TSB operates a mostly flexible model adapted for its own circumstances – Pearson has access to an investment fund and can be reasonably sure that he will have work for the six staff dedicated to ventures. He also has strong support from top management and a good relationship with finance. Even with these, however, his Strategic Ventures is one-third of the size of those at Kudu (Chapter 1), Royal & SunAlliance and Cyntec (Chapter 13).

How big should a unit be? In spite of Roche Diagnostics' success – its venture unit is the only single-person operation that we have come across – two people seems a sensible minimum. Two staff alleviates the risk of one leaving and allows the unit to cope with a sudden rush of work, holidays and illness. From a business perspective, it usually enables a more balanced and reliable selection of early projects, as two views are generally better than one.

In terms of a maximum, consider the following arithmetic. An experienced venture unit professional in a flexible unit can mentor around five average $100 000 projects per year through the Start stage and two average $500 000 projects through Seed. Adding in overhead, salary and the costs of attracting ideas, and assuming that larger ventures require more venture unit effort per dollar than the average, then a figure of one venture unit executive per $2 million of venture unit budget is a useful benchmark. In Chapter 5 we said that $5 million of venture unit budget buys the option to invest in cumulative revenue opportunities of between $160 million and $500 million. This translates to $65 million to $200 million per venture unit employee.

A venture unit of 10 staff operating on the flexible model can generate total annual recurring revenue opportunities of the order of $1 billion during each year of its operation (assuming that appropriate opportunities exist). Some proportion of this fails to win investment or wins external investment, thereby alleviating the investment burden on the parent firm, but the volume is still vast. As few firms have the capacity to sustain business creation investment at that level, we suggest that a venture unit of 10 is the maximum for all but the biggest firms. The precise size of the unit depends, of course, on the level of opportunities facing the firm.

Funding is almost always centrally provided, and must be if P & L-focused divisions are not to complain. At Lloyds TSB funding comes from the Group centre, and at Shell funding for the Gamechanger programme within its Exploration and Production division is located in central budgets that are agreed annually between the centre and the operating units.

Staffing

When the board of British American Tobacco decided to form a venture unit it turned to a pair of senior management executives with a mix of contrasting characteristics: young but seasoned; innovative but clear-thinking and disciplined. Phil Colman was a senior manager in the company's IT group, while Jeremy Pike had been General Manager of BAT's Kenya business. This combined an executive who understood the possibilities presented by new technology with a seasoned businessman.

BAT has 80 000 staff worldwide and identifies those with senior management potential early in their career with the firm. These are known throughout the company as 'listers'. Pike and Colman wanted to hire a talented team to run their 'Imagine' (idea generation and selection) and 'Evolution' (idea development and rollout) sub-groups. According to Colman: 'We looked for people who would do anything but telling a team of people what to do. We needed a team of very capable and knowledgeable people who could work with uncertainty, were creative and whose sleeves rolled-up.' Pike and Colman decided, therefore, to select only 'listers'.

Getting the right people to staff a venture unit is not straight-forward. The necessary skills are uncommon within large organizations, and many venture unit executives have to descend a steep learning curve. The optimal characteristics for venture unit managers are:

■ Wide knowledge of the company, its assets and its strategic agenda and processes.

■ An entrepreneurial attitude and an understanding of entrepreneurs.

■ The ability to deal with pressure situations and unorthodox people.

■ The ability to communicate with the CEO and junior executives alike.

■ A wide array of marketing, technical and general management skills.

■ A strong personal network inside and outside the company.

Consultants

Consultants are useful if they do what the customer wants and not what the customer does not yet know it does not want! An external viewpoint can bring a valuable perspective to a corporate initiative and specialist knowledge can be invaluable. Lonnie Shoff of Roche Diagnostics says, 'The only external consultants we have engaged for venture development have been for market research. One consultant rolled up his sleeves recently to produce a business plan and then decided to join the company to carry on with the project.'

However, venture unit managers need to be careful when using venturing consultants. BAT's Phil Colman characterizes the problem this way. 'I think consultants should come, consult, transfer knowledge and leave. But all too often they came, multiplied, charged and eventually left with the knowledge.' Tim Forrest at Powergen says 'Don't let them get entrenched in the engine room or you will end up with a consultant on every project'. On the other hand, he adds, 'they can provide delivery drive, project planning skills and a calm approach to the ebb and flow of the individual venture'.

At the beginning of their lives, venture units need help in three separate areas: processes for generating ideas; processes for selecting and developing ideas; and assistance with actual venture development. We have encountered several firms who have wasted a great deal of money on process consultants in this area because they have not specified which of the three deliverables the consultancy is to produce and because they do not know how to manage process consultants. Business creation consultancies tend to specialize in one or both of the process areas; most of them, however, also want to sell into venture development because such engagements can go on for a long time and produce the dependency that most consultancy firms crave.

Process consultants, therefore, are useful for teaching techniques to the venture unit. They are poor for venture development, where industry and business discipline specialists are better positioned to add value. Using individual consultants – market research experts, business plan writers, industry experts – is an ideal way to test and recruit good staff (as we saw at Roche Diagnostics) for the parent company and the venture when it receives investment.

Positioning

We have already said that business creation is deeply linked to strategy and the remainder of business development. If the venture unit sits too far away from these functions it risks operating at odds with the company and suffering eventual closure. Ideally, the venture unit is a peer to the M & A group, the venture capital function and the R & D development group. Only in this way is the venture unit able to ensure that it selects ventures that are consistent with strategy and that fit inside a portfolio of businesses that the other groups are developing.

Vince Forlenza at Becton Dickinson echoes the importance of these connections: 'Although all the groups, VC, R & D and Incubator, operate independently, they all understand the value of co-operation and they work in unison. Each reports to the venture review board, which also owns the corporate strategy and implements it in relation to the range of opportunities that is brought before it from any of the three groups'.

OPERATION

In Chapter 5 we said that the venture unit services management and entrepreneurs by controlling risk and costs, by keeping business creation away from routine operating activities, and by providing venture teams with freedom, resources, help and security. It runs the managed market and, as markets are neutral and transparent, so must the venture unit be. Further, as service providers and managers, venture unit staff must be helpful and trustworthy. We show in Chapter 8 how these characteristics help the unit to generate and attract ideas from all quarters.

Managing the pipeline

As time goes by, ventures under development fill up the pipeline. As anybody who has managed a logistics operation knows, pipelines have a maximum throughput and are riddled with bottlenecks. Pipeline management is therefore an art.

The first projects that the unit takes on can make or break it, so the more care and attention paid to these the better the chances of business creation's survival. Small is beautiful at the beginning when capabilities are low and a working relationship with the strategy function may not yet be established.

The best initial projects are close to the core, cheap and deliver revenue quickly. Tim Forrest at Powergen explains: 'Have success early on in the portfolio. We had one at Powergen which rose 3–4 months after the start. The treacle [middle management] sees it and thinks it's sensible. It is vital that the treacle doesn't see the first ventures and think that they are a waste of time.' The simplest approach is the reuse of an existing asset into a new market. This incurs little technical development costs and if the existing sales and support channels are also reused the prospects of large new revenues at little incremental costs can be exciting.

Over time, bigger ventures become necessary if the unit is to make a difference for the firm. Rick Wills of British Airways observes that sustained success requires a mixed portfolio – some quick hits, but also some bigger and higher-risk projects. Victor Prodonoff from Embraer, the Brazilian aerospace group, sums it up, 'Be bold, but not too bold – start small, succeed and then build'.

Overall, there are three tricks to managing the venture pipeline:

- Keep the pipeline evenly stocked along its length so that ventures emerge for investment at evenly-spaced intervals.

- Maintain a mixture of big and small and risky and non-risky ventures in order to satisfy constituencies variously demanding scale, adventurousness, economy and caution. Go for small, fast ventures early on.

■ Maintain a mix of core and non-core ventures in order to be able to satisfy constituencies variously demanding expansion and focus. Concentrate on core ventures during the early stages unless the unit's mission is explicitly non-core.

Communications

One venture unit manager told us that relationships between top management, middle management and the broad mass of staff in her company are like those between the equivalent classes in society. Middle management, she said, is like the middle class – aspirational, grasping and sensitive to small differences in status. She characterized her venture unit as a link between her firm's top management and its staff that effectively bypassed the elaborate power structures – budgets, procedures, hiring and firing, reporting lines – operated by middle management. This venture unit manager had the right to pull any member of the firm's staff into a new venture and had first call on legal and human resources time. In spite of her strong connections with senior executives, she spends half of her time battling with middle management.

The key to dealing with these battles is communications. If organized and managed correctly, business creation brings strategic and financial benefits, does not cost much to run, and positions the firm for growth and renewal as we have seen. Continual communication of these benefits, the status of individual ventures and how the development and selection process works, helps prevent rumour, myth and legend spreading and helps to establish the venture unit as neutral, transparent and trustworthy rather than elitist, remote and irrelevant.

Monitoring progress

Business creation is hard to measure. Strategic benefits come in the long term and are difficult to express financially, while financial benefits (value creation) also take a long time to flow through and are often impossible to measure within five years. Even at that point, what happens if a successful new business unit is reintegrated into the firm's line structure when it starts to make a profit? How can a firm judge the value of that business against the investment it made before the venture turned cash flow positive? Few firms follow the example set by Prudential and IPO their ventures, for good strategic reason. The best ventures are core ventures, and the core is not for sale.

Executives from Intel Capital consider 10 years to be an appropriate horizon for a venture capital fund. Corporate business creation is no different. But how can the firm measure the success of its business creation activities from year to year? Input measurements are no good (if they were then Kudu Ventures would have been deemed successful). Fixed funds and budgets are just an invitation to spend money on second-rate ideas. Output measures are necessary, but what outputs?

Let us return to the flows within the business creation architecture and see where measurements can be made. Venture units turn money, ideas and people into ventures ready for investment. Some of these go on to secure investment, and some go on to generate revenue and ultimately move into profit. A few are sold or, like Prudential's Egg, are floated. The following three measures look at venture unit efficiency and success without causing perverse incentives, and can be calculated within the first 3 years of the start of a business creation programme before any assessment of value creation can be made.

The first and most immediately calculable is a measure of the *efficiency* with which venture unit budget is turned into investment opportunity. Budget is easy to track, while the opportunity's scale can be measured by any of NPV, investment requirement and revenue exposure, as cited in the venture's business plan. Of these, revenue exposure is best because the greater a revenue opportunity the more work usually goes into researching and proving it. The multiplier of between 30 and 100 that we indicated earlier is a useful, but admittedly broad, benchmark.

The second is the *investment ratio* – the proportion of investment opportunities that win investment, regardless of source. This has the useful benefit of encouraging the venture unit and venture review board to kill bad ideas at an early stage so that they don't drive this ratio down. The third is a measure of *venture survival* over time. What proportion of ventures have lasted 1, 2 and more years? Clearly, ventures mutate after investment – business models and strategies change – but a basic measure of whether funded ventures are still operating provides a strong indication of the success or otherwise of the venture unit.

These measures are heavily outweighed in importance by value creation and are unsatisfactory in comparison to the frequency and visibility of the chief indicators of company success or failure – revenues, earnings and market value. The absence of such indicators means that, for business creation to succeed, CEOs must recognize and value its interim strategic benefits (hence the questions in the business creation audit). These strategic benefits – readiness to exploit growth and renewal opportunities, options to invest, the business creation capability itself, live but loss-making investments in key areas – sustain the activity in the short to medium term while financial benefits come through. Without this CEO support, the (generic) CFOs will eventually get their way in the eternal jousting with their Strategy and Business Development counterparts.

CONCLUSION

In this chapter we have made seven major points about the venture unit:

■ Venture units exist to build and manage a business creation capability. If, according to the business creation audit, the firm has a strong capability already in place then a dedicated venture unit may not be necessary.

■ Venture units are most efficient when small and adaptive to the level of opportunities. Somewhere between two and ten professional staff is suitable for most firms.

- Venture unit staff are usually high-quality executives with extensive business experience, a good knowledge of the firm and empathy for entrepreneurship.

- Venture units operate a managed market in ideas, money and people and, like markets, should be neutral and transparent. In order to arbitrate between management and staff, they should be helpful and trustworthy.

- Maintaining a diverse venture pipeline helps the venture unit satisfy various constituencies across the firm. Quick wins come first, though.

- Value creation is the only true measure of business creation, but is hard to measure for many years.

- This lack of measurability explains much of the vulnerability of business creation. To compensate, the CEO must give extra weight to the strategic benefits of business creation and back Strategy and Business Development against Finance.

8 Sense

Imagine that a CEO wants to recruit a new business management team. Her first tasks are to define the responsibilities of the new group and write a set of job descriptions for the manager and the staff. Then she launches a search inside and outside the company, perhaps with a professional recruiter. Slowly, a long list of résumés build up on her desk. Then the sifting begins. She, the recruiter and HR come up with some criteria and use them to whittle the pile down to a dozen well-qualified and suitable people. Each of these is interviewed once by HR and the recruiter and a short list of six selected. Second-round interviews with other executives reduce the list to two. The CEO has dinner with each and makes the final selection.

Gathering business ideas requires the same process of definition, outreach, sifting and selection. Some firms prefer to leave idea generation to strategy and business development specialists, or even to top management. This is cheap and quick, but can result in the loss of valuable insights from customer-facing staff in sales and marketing and from outside the company altogether. In this chapter we describe how venture units define what they want, how they generate and attract ideas and how they 'sift through the mud to get to the gold'.

STARTING-UP

Wise business people know that the answer to any question depends on the phrasing of the question and why it is being asked. Before starting any idea solicitation exercise the venture unit has to define a strategic context, a selection process and a venture development process.

Consider the case of a Boston-based financial services firm. In early 2001, it began a scheme to attract 'innovative and transformational' ideas from employees. The project enjoyed CEO support and was run by the Head of Leadership Development within the HR group, who decided to run a company-wide ideas contest. Employees sent in hundreds of submissions. Several of the ideas, though, suggested changes to the reception area at the base of the building and others were about the types of plants dotted around the office. In fact, when the team had reviewed the complete set of submissions, not one of the ideas was of value.

The manager sought some advice, and found that in order to attract good ideas she needed to establish both a business context and an idea sifting process. In particular, she had to tell staff what types of ideas she was looking for and what she intended to do with those selected. The group took these conclusions on board and scaled back the effort in order to focus on a few target sources. For its next solicitation exercise, it developed a set of clear criteria, and was pleased with the small but appropriate set of responses that this produced.

Just as bad money chases out good, so bad ideas chase out good ones. A venture unit has a delicate path to tread: the more context and direction given, the more refined the response, but the lower the chances of a diamond in the rough. The less that is stipulated in advance, the more the rough obscures the single diamond.

Context

The Boston example suggests the key questions. The first, and easiest, is the business domain: within divisions, between divisions, completely non-core, or across divisions? In practice, the areas covered by a venture unit depend to a great extent on where it resides within the firm. ChevronTexaco, for instance, stated that it wanted ideas only in new or adjacent markets and specifically not in core markets. The unit at Roche sits in Roche Diagnostics and, no surprise, covers diagnostics but not pharmaceuticals. In firms where the venture unit works alongside group strategy, such as Lloyds TSB and Diageo, the remit generally covers the core of the firm as well as non-core ideas. A good example of a central co-ordinated business approach is at Sainsbury's, whose business strategy indicates favoured areas but where the unit does not exclude ideas from outside those areas. However, as we have seen, the point is to stipulate the areas of interest in advance.

The second question is the business model. Does the unit want product or process enhancements or new products or services? Most companies, but not all, limit their business creation initiatives to new products or services that require a business creation, rather than a business extension approach. This is for good reason, as existing business units generally do business extension and process enhancements.

The third question is source. Ideas come from management, staff and outside the firm. As new business-creation systems start up it usually becomes obvious that there is never any shortage of them within or outside the organization. Raphael Offer from Diageo says, 'Ideas are a dime a dozen. A clear process to find the best ideas, orchestrated by the right people, is the most valuable element.'

Most venture units source ideas primarily from within the firm and only get around to outside ideas when the internal flow has dried up. Rick Wills from BA strongly advocates external ideas because BA Enterprises developed non-core ideas. 'There are three sources of ideas', he says, 'Two are not of great value for corporate venturing. Staff suggestions are best handled by the HR department, for example where people in the core business can get rewarded for core business improvement ideas. Brainstorming can sometimes work, but the best ideas come from the outside.' Cisco, though, is a good example of the more standard approach that delivers ideas in both core and non-core areas. Paul Shreve, head of business development for Cisco in

Europe, estimates that about half of the proposals his group receives originate from within the company's business units.

Sources

Staff, management and outsiders come at this from different positions because they have different expectations of the venture unit and different motivations for putting forward their ideas. Entrepreneurs are motivated by some mixture of money, experience, fame, power, escape, interest or driven by a creative urge. Some of these are positive and some negative. Should the would-be entrepreneur manifest a desire for escape, fame and power then further investigation may be necessary. Creativity and interest sometimes result in a desire to play around, perhaps with a product technology. Money is an odd one: why is the entrepreneur still with the firm? Lastly, the desire for experience and learning is the best sign of the seriousness of intent and the self-possession that define the successful corporate entrepreneur. This desire drives the essential bargain between firm and entrepreneur, as we describe in Chapter 12.

Management ideas come from committees, strategy consultants, bankers and from senior managers themselves. The problem with management ideas, though, is that they have a habit of becoming corporate imperatives regardless of their value. Many are deal-led, with the business opportunity wrapped up in the execution method – usually an acquisition. Those directed at the venture unit require careful handling in its early days. Block the idea, and life may be difficult at the next funding discussion. Accept the idea, and the flow of ideas from staff and outside may slow down. The best choice by far is to work through the idea selection process using the selection criteria that we have outlined.

Outsiders, such as customers and open market entrepreneurs, sometimes have a better perspective of the company's assets and their uses. However, external ideas tend to involve intellectual property, especially where the proposal replicates an idea already being explored by the firm or which resides in the company's core business. Nokia advises the outsider to visit its legal department before it considers the proposal. The optimum solution is to create a standard approach for ideas from outside that clearly establishes the firm's approach and allows the entrepreneur some leeway over IP ownership.

The best ideas tend to come from two sources. Internally, from middle managers with 5 or more years of experience within the company or its industry, good business skills, an understanding of the company's assets, an ability to think strategically and a good network among the firm's customers. Externally, from entrepreneurs and other firms. They usually know something about the marketplace that the firm does not know, have something the firm does not have, and have approached the firm for a reason.

STIMULATING IDEA CREATION

There are many possible approaches to stimulating new idea creation, ranging from a one-off speaker session to a comprehensive programme of workshops. Generally speaking, the more comprehensive the programme, the more effective it will be at stimulating ideas (see Example 8.1). However, it is important to bear in mind before getting started that the vast majority of ideas ends up being rejected. At Ericsson, for example, despite the existence of what Tomas Ulin calls 'a strong family culture' and an environment where 'people want to see ideas happen', the selecting board assesses ideas ruthlessly. According to Ulin, it is easy to create a 'constituency of the disappointed' across the company. The remedy is to acknowledge this in all communications as an inevitable fact of life that does not reflect poorly on the people with the idea.

Example 8.1   Stimulating new ideas at Royal & SunAlliance

In September 1999, Stuart Degg, then Strategy Director at Royal & SunAlliance, decided that the company needed an innovation academy. The feeling at the company was that the time had come to 'challenge the norms' and 'to find better ways to serve customers that don't sit nicely within the core'. Degg secured the support of CEO Bob Mendelsohn and sent an email to all 54 000 employees. In it, he exhorted them to 'liberate the capabilities of the firm' and to 'come and join me'.

The email resulted in the formation of a 15-strong 'Hothouse' team, which subsequently met experts inside and outside Royal & SunAlliance to develop a picture of the drivers of change in the industry and to collect ideas for exploiting them commercially. The group then ran an internal communications campaign and created a system for generating and sorting ideas. This process included running short sessions where participants were encouraged to create concepts and then review them with the group.

The process delivered a flow of over 1000 ideas into a newly established business, Global Ventures. Of these, 400 were subjected to initial investigation, 40 to detailed desk research and seven were developed into new businesses.

Managed events

Managed events, such as Royal & SunAlliance's Hothouse, are good for marketing a venture unit and its business creation process inside and outside the firm. They also help encourage creative thinking both at the events and afterwards. However, to avoid generating endless reams of irrelevant ideas, Royal & SunAlliance's Hothouse format incorporated a selection element to steer participants to strategic fit and financial attractiveness. Another way to achieve the same end is to work-up a definition of the company's assets and analyse how they add value for one of the company's businesses. This naturally focuses attendees' creativity on ideas related to those assets.

The five methods below vary by how interactive and how targeted they are. Interactive sessions are good for encouraging creativity and working up ideas, whereas direct methods help the venture unit sell itself as a vehicle for the best opportunities.

Brainstorming

Interactive idea-generation sessions built around a broad business theme are suitable for generating large numbers of ideas quickly and getting staff and management used to thinking openly and creatively. Good facilitation is central to the success of this type of event, so that criticism is constructive and participants work quickly. At British American Tobacco (BAT), venture unit manager Phil Colman worked with Ernst & Young to produce a one-off event called 'E-Forum' for 40 senior executives from around BAT's global organization. Using techniques unfamiliar to most of these executives, E&Y and Colman focused the event on the business opportunities that the firm faced, building up a list of ideas and then ranking them 'Now', 'Soon' or 'Later'.

Workshops

Interactive process and skills education sessions built around specific ideas help develop these ideas into business proposals and teach participants about the methods to select and develop ideas. They also have a strong word-of-mouth effect as attendees pass on details to colleagues and encourage them to use the venture unit as a vehicle for developing ideas.

These workshops usually operate over a period of days and are often orientated around specific business issues or existing ideas, identified in advance by the venture unit, which also runs the event. Participants can include external industry experts and are usually selected rather than self-selected. During the sessions, participants are divided into groups which then work-up specific aspects of one idea, such as customer proposition and business model, presenting each aspect back to all the other participants for feedback. Finally, each team presents its proposal to a selection board composed of senior executives and external venture capitalists. The board uses the selection criteria to choose a winner, and the venture unit then takes this and other suitable proposals through its formal idea screening process.

Competitions

Venture units use competitions to stimulate widespread interest in idea creation and to fill the ideas pot. However, they are high-profile and expensive, and are not for the unwary. As we saw from the Boston example, the minimum set of prerequisites includes rules governing who can enter, details of the selection process (including the identity of the selectors), a line on intellectual property, some indication of preferred business areas, and a statement of the process for developing selected ideas. If managed well they create a large volume of intellectual property in a short time, and they can be highly effective in uncovering ideas that match the company's requirements.

Speaker sessions

Speeches by experts give employees an opportunity to hear a successful person's story and motivate them to reveal a suppressed business idea. The most useful speakers are experienced and successful corporate entrepreneurs. External experts, such as venture capitalists, open market entrepreneurs and business angels, provide an inside look at what goes on outside. The worst speakers are usually corporate executives declaiming the official line about encouraging innovation.

Targeting

Direct venture unit approaches to selected individuals is a good way for the venture unit to supplement the random flow that comes from brainstorming, workshops and speeches. Many managers of R&D units, business units and marketing groups encounter opportunities, while the fringes of the firm, sales and subsidiaries are often thick with good ideas and entrepreneurial talent.

Open mechanisms

Open mechanisms, such as websites, broadcast information and provide an alternative means of interaction between the venture unit and potential entrepreneurs. Typically, open mechanisms are used in combination with managed events (see Example 8.2).

Example 8.2   Open sensing mechanisms at Roche Diagnostics

Roche Diagnostics has generated over 6000 ideas from the division's 17 000 staff since its inception in January 2001. Although not all the ideas submitted have been germane, the group has worked on 34 ventures, of which three are generating revenues. One successful venture is mydoc, a medical self-diagnosis service, which generated revenue after 11 months.

Lonnie Shoff uses a set of methods to generate ideas. The first, 'Voice My Idea', is the venture unit website, and Shoff estimates that 70 per cent of submitted ideas arrive this way. The next is formal ideation sessions, which typically involve a mixture of insiders and outsiders focused on a topic, such as 'Ways to simplify health-care systems'. She also solicits ideas from Roche Diagnostics' regional organizations, such as its country business units, and from business development. Lastly, there is random submission of ideas.

Website

Venture unit managers generally advertise their services and processes through the company intranet. This is a good way to describe the people in the venture unit and the business creation architecture. The most important of these are the selection system and who carries it out, the venture development process, the terms of employee transfer, IPR issues and how ventures are terminated.

Roche Diagnostics and Powergen include idea submission templates. A light touch is necessary here, as forms can repel and intimidate. A good approach is to ask questions rather than provide headings and not to insist on answers to every question.

Community

The Spark unit at Powergen has tried to create a business creation community. With articles in the company staff magazine, the chart on the wall showing the status of projects in the venture pipeline, a video playing in common areas of its offices and 'day in the life of a venture executive' workshops, Spark communicates success and encourages participation.

OVERCOMING OBSTACLES TO IDEA GENERATION

Many idea creation schemes never get off the ground because cultural obstacles prevent individuals from revealing or developing their ideas. Successful venture units overcome these obstacles by being neutral, transparent, helpful and trustworthy.

Cynicism

This can destroy business creation within a firm. Often the result of previous failure, it can exist at all levels within the company. Transparency in the selection and the venture development process indicates that there is no catch, and openness to any idea from any source indicates the absence of a hidden agenda.

Mistrust

Some employees are unsure how they will be treated when proposing an idea. By demonstrating its neutrality, a venture unit can build up a reputation for trustworthiness even while it has to reject a large majority of ideas.

Fear of failure

Failure is an integral part of venturing and is a sign of a healthy process. Some would-be entrepreneurs, though, may be unwilling to risk career, self-esteem and reputation. By being helpful, a venture unit reduces the risk of failure, and by being trustworthy it convinces the entrepreneur to agree to the employment bargain that it operates for venture teams.

Lack of reward

Corporate entrepreneurs can be motivated by money. Some firms operate equity-based compensation schemes for internal entrepreneurs, but a better bargain in corporate business creation is based on the learning and experience for both sides, with rewards for the entrepreneur coming much later if the venture is successful and creates business value.

Management hostility

Line managers can be hostile towards ventures that take their staff away. Some try to prevent staff leaving, but this usually leads to the employee changing roles or leaving the company. By involving the line manager at an early stage and using senior management influence selectively, a venture unit can get around this obstacle.

HANDLING IDEAS

In venturing there is no such thing as a bad idea. An idea may be weak on every single criterion, nothing to do with the company, and appallingly described, but it is still not bad. It is just something that, regrettably, the venture unit 'cannot proceed with at this time because there are several other opportunities more appropriate for the firm.' A venture unit is playing with fire when evaluating other people's ideas, and the only way to avoid being scalded is to operate a response system that evinces the transparency, neutrality and other attributes described above. Such a system should work for ideas of any size from both the CEO and most junior member of staff

Initial response

Entrepreneurs are not patient people, but the unit may want to consult colleagues and outsiders and check whether a similar idea is being developed elsewhere in the firm. A quick but formal initial response within 24 hours thanks the submitter and promises a decision within a certain period. A reminder of the decision system and how it works impresses on the entrepreneur the neutrality and transparency of the venturing system. This is also a good time to ask the entrepreneur some questions about her idea to allow better evaluation.

Evaluating ideas

At least two members of the venture unit evaluate the idea using the published criteria, then discuss and resolve their differences so that each can present a united front when discussing the decision later. Some ideas are unsuitable in a way that is difficult to establish using criteria. Where this is the case, the unit can express its doubts to the entrepreneur but agree to put the project in Start with no budget to allow both the entrepreneur and the venture unit to work through them. If the idea does pass the criteria, a meeting is necessary. If it does not, then the idea goes into a 'dormant ideas' database for audit purposes and in case it comes round again or the entrepreneur calls the CEO.

Rejecting ideas

Most ideas are rejected, but Harry Berry of BT's Brightstar venture unit says: 'Don't kill the passion. People and their energy are central to making a company effective.' The trick is to help the entrepreneur understand why the idea does not pass one or more of the criteria. A killer question that the entrepreneur cannot answer puts the onus on the entrepreneur to answer it and places the venture unit in a win–win situation. A poor answer confirms the initial view, and a good answer means that the idea may be worth developing and that the entrepreneur has some of the persistence and dedication necessary to succeed. In any case, a negative response should hold out the possibility of the idea coming round again and of the entrepreneur sending in more ideas.

Meeting the entrepreneur

At the first meeting with the entrepreneur with a good idea, the venture unit assesses the person's commitment, intelligence, skills and industry expertise. At the same time, it seeks to communicate trustworthiness and offers help. On the other hand, venture evaluation is a constant part of the process and, for transparency's sake, the entrepreneur should know that his venture can be terminated at any point. At this point, entrepreneurs need to know about the development process, intellectual property, employment terms and conditions, the risks and consequences of failure, the help available and, finally, the circumstances in which ventures can be terminated. These together constitute a contract between the entrepreneur and the venture unit and belong in an entrepreneurs' information pack that the venture unit may wish to put together.

Setting initial goals

The best way to generate mutual understanding is to start working together on the project. The unit sets the agenda by asking the six Batch 1 questions that we listed in Chapter 6, and the entrepreneur works up the business opportunity by answering them with the unit's help. This way, the entrepreneur sees what the unit can do for him, and the unit sees what the entrepreneur can do for himself.

Two weeks is usually sufficient for the venture team (no longer 'the entrepreneur') to produce this piece of work, and the speed and competence with which the team does this is useful information for the unit. The result is a presentation by the team to a review group from the venture unit for a decision on whether the idea progresses to the Start stage.

CONCLUSION

In this chapter we have made five major points about the Sense stage:

■   Before embarking on an idea solicitation exercise, a venture unit must define the context in which it is operating. This is made up of the business areas in which ideas should reside, the types of business model, sources of ideas and the processes for selecting and developing them.

■   All business creation ideas go through the venture unit (or its equivalent), which is responsible for stimulating and attracting ideas.

■   There are many obstacles to idea formation in large firms. The four vital venture unit attributes – neutrality, transparency, trustworthiness and helpfulness – together overcome them.

■   Handling would-be entrepreneurs is an art. No ideas are bad. Gentle use of evaluation criteria helps explain why an idea cannot go forward.

■   An initial 2-week definition project helps the venture unit and the venture team get to know each other and drives the decision on whether to put the venture into Start.

9 Start

Start begins when the venture unit has heard the entrepreneur's presentation and has decided to proceed with the venture. Here, the venture development process begins to accelerate. The main output of this stage is a proposal to go to the next stage – Seed – that proves the Batch 1 marketing and strategy claims made during Sense to the necessary degree. This stage is short, at most a few months long, and not particularly intensive.

The most important activity in Start is research to establish a product concept and matching customer proposition. For example, Diageo started a venture in summer 2000 called Guinness Good Times, which sought to give travellers to Ireland a good time through a set of Guinness-branded travel services. Diageo knew little about the travel industry, but the idea was promising enough to be deemed worth an initial £30 000. Example 9.1 describes the first part of this case, and the rest of the story is told as this and the next chapter progress.

Example 9.1 Guinness Good Times (1)

Diageo's Guinness Good Times (GGT) venture started in summer 2000 at an idea-generation session. Staff from subsidiary Guinness had long searched for business ideas that would stretch the world-renowned and immensely valuable Guinness brand further into leisure to generate returns from that area and from new Guinness drinkers. The idea was to offer visitors to Ireland a Guinness experience. Built around the country's long-standing association with the 'black stuff', it would provide visitors information, guidance and help while bathing them in the Guinness brand. The company had recently opened a sparkling new venue at the Guinness Brewery in Dublin. Named 'Storehouse', it is a museum, restaurant and Guinness emporium rolled into one. Some synergy seemed to exist between this and the GGT concept.

Diageo had just set up a New Business Ventures group to take forward ideas such as this. The new group reported to the Strategy Director, and strategy executive Rupert Markland took over the job of developing the idea (originally entitled 'Irish Travel Series presented by Guinness') with an initial budget of £30 000. However, few people in Diageo knew about the travel industry, and Markland embarked on the long trek uphill with a plan to answer some basic questions. The customer proposition was to give travellers to Ireland a good time, but what did this mean? Who would be interested in this and why? Did the Guinness brand, one of Diageo's most valuable assets – 'Power, goodness and communion' – add any value in the travel business? These were the questions that Markland needed to answer quickly.

On occasions, a proposal is so well formed during Sense that it can bypass Start and go straight into Seed. This happens when the questions usually covered in Start have already been answered. With such a low degree of uncertainty about the viability and scale of the venture, there is no point in it drifting through Start.

Team and budget

The big costs at this stage are external industry consultants and any market surveys. The remaining work is strategic thinking and desk research, both of which are relatively low cost. Start usually costs somewhere between 0.2 and 0.6 per cent of the revenue opportunity, implying that a $50 million annual revenue opportunity project costs between $100 000 and $300 000. For larger ideas with external industry consultants and a big market survey across borders with translation, travel and so on, the percentage drops to the lower end of this range.

Once the venture unit has decided to proceed with the idea, the entrepreneur arrives at a watershed where he or she becomes part of a venture team. At this point it all begins to get serious and some formality is required in the. relationship between the venture team and the unit. Some entrepreneurs back out at this stage. In this case, the venture unit should easily be able to find someone to undertake the Start stage. If the entrepreneur is from a technology or corporate services background then he may need some help from a marketing executive or an industry specialist.

Employment

Venture teams can be nervous about embarking on a venture while still employed in other full-time roles. They may be thinking about quitting their jobs and concentrating full-time on the venture. At this stage, though, as there is still considerable uncertainty about whether the project will make it into Seed, quitting is not good practice.

Several venture units have experienced reluctance on the part of line managers to release staff. 'Taking people from operations can be very tricky,' says Victor Prodonoff at Embraer in Brazil, 'the market is very tight for high quality technical people and the secondment or removal of staff can be very painful'. When Royal & SunAlliance formed its venture group in 2000, Stuart Degg ran into all kinds of problems securing the permanent release of the 15 staff that he wanted.

The line manager can ultimately be either the greatest supporter or the worst obstacle for the venture, and the manner in which he or she is approached may determine how successful the venture becomes. Deals are possible. For instance, the individual can work on the venture outside working hours or for 1 day a week within working hours. Another option is for the venture unit to pay for a temporary replacement for the person for a few months. In any case, an unambiguous and careful method of working with line managers pre-empts trouble.

Termination

The venture unit can terminate the venture at any point. Consequences for venture team members at this stage are few as they have remained in their jobs, but forewarning the team of this rule forearms the unit against adverse reaction. When a venture is stopped, a sense of openness and transparency is best cultivated with explanations couched in terms of the company's selection criteria.

Help

The members of the venture team may not previously have had to deliver on such tight deadlines closely linked to their personal performance. Most venture units (e.g. Powergen) allocate a mentor. Others (e.g. Lloyds TSB) allocate staff. Mentors need to tread a fine balance with the team, as it is easy for them to become too involved with the project and to lose perspective on its feasibility. The mentor's role is therefore to remain separate from the team and ensure that it is protected and served as needed.

MARKETING AND PRODUCT WORK

This is a time of flux for the team, as it has to distil the idea into its barest parts and decide what to include and what to leave behind. The team needs to get to grips with what has to be done rather than what it would like to do, and this can be quite a hard process.

A Los Angeles-based television company operated an internal ideas scheme and, in mid-1999, three middle managers decided to take up the challenge. The company owned a video and film archive from which it sold footage to programme makers and researchers, delivering videos by mail. Although profitable, it was a small business, and the three managers felt that the archive was underused. They came up with an idea for a new product technology by which customers could access the archive online and splice together segments using editing software, and after an initial review were awarded $40 000.

The team set to work and uncovered some encouraging high-level commercial data on the use of video archives. Then they elected to test the venture's feasibility with a prototype of the delivery technology. Once the prototype was finished, the team prepared a jazzy show for the company's venture review board that consisted of a lengthy prototype demonstration and an extravagant presentation. The review board was unconvinced and rejected the idea for further funding. It found that there was insufficient market research data to prove that there was a substantial paying market for the concept. Secondly, when it asked about the concept's strategic fit, it found that this had been overlooked by the team.

Most businesses start with a product concept. As soon as the Start stage gets going, however, product work scales down and marketing work scales up. The adverse case of the Los Angeles film archive indicates what has to be produced in the Start stage. The first and most important is what the product does and for whom and why (product concept and customer proposition). Next, can it in theory be produced and delivered? Then, what is the scale of the opportunity in revenue terms, and what is the shape of the industry and its incumbents?

Product concept and customer proposition

Developing an effective customer proposition is crucial to the success of the venture and may be the hardest piece for the venture team to deliver. 'Every week a proposal appears that is a great product, but one without any customers,' says Mark Klopp of Eastman Chemical. We too have come across many product ideas that have no customer proposition and barely contain a product concept. What are these elusive properties?

Let us take the case of GM's OnStar. The idea behind this venture is to place a combination of a Global Positioning System (GPS) receiver and a mobile data device in a car so that it knows where it is and can relay its position. So, does that mean the product concept is a GPS telephone combo and the customer proposition is to tell the driver where he or she is?

No it does not. A product concept is a high-level description of what the product actually does, its specific features and functions and how it works in the hands of the user. A customer proposition describes what customers are doing when using the product, the interests they are pursuing, their activities and objectives, and it defines how the product adds value to these, perhaps by helping them do something they could not do before or by making an existing activity easier or cheaper. Often it includes the definition of the customers, perhaps by age, nationality or gender, in ways that help define their activities and fit them into a group.

A customer proposition is often best developed through a story. Consider this one for OnStar: 'I am in my car on the way to a wedding but a thief has stolen my side mirror. It is illegal to drive with no side mirror, so I have to get another one now. But I do not want to make a detour or spend ages looking around. Is there a shop that sells this item within a few miles of my route?' The product concept here is 'provides real-time consumer item location and direction information' and the customer proposition is 'saves time for a driver in a hurry'. The customer proposition and the product concept relate to each other just as do features and benefits.

There are thousands of stories like this – they depend on what the person is doing and where they are – and they boil down to scores of paired elements that together comprise the customer proposition and the product concept.

Researching proposition and concept

The only way to research proposition and concept is to brainstorm them with colleagues and ask potential customers what they think, using representations such as prototypes and storyboards that display the product idea cheaply and accurately. After a few iterations the venture team can see if it all coheres and the venture is viable.

> **Example 9.2   Guinness Good Times (2)**
>
> At Diageo, Rupert Markland ran two tours of Dublin pubs hosted by a Guinness ambassador to test the Guinness association and the pub tour part of the product concept. This research showed that discovery, information, safety, memorableness, relaxation and friendly service were the six most important customer needs. These matched the ideas for the product that Markland and his colleagues from Guinness had generated. Apart from a trip to Storehouse and pub tours, they included golf, visits to Guinness family sites, guides to historical Dublin, visitor packs and taxis back to the hotel at the end of the evening.

Rupert Markland's product research detailed in Example 9.2 produced excellent detail on the various elements of his concept, and he later used focus groups to further develop the idea. Potential customers are invited, and usually paid, to attend a brainstorming meeting where a moderator takes them through a presentation of a new product concept. The moderator then asks members of the group to express their opinions about what they have heard and encourages them to discuss their responses with each other. The venture team sits in an adjacent room behind a one-way mirror and listens with gritted teeth to its product concept being lampooned.

Scaling the proposition

Again, the only way to do this is to ask potential customers. A separate survey is necessary because questions about pricing and interest in purchasing do not blend well with the interactive brainstorming that goes on at product concept sessions. Once the concept and proposition are worked-up, the team can try a short questionnaire on a suitable number of potential customers (Example 9.3).

Example 9.3   Guinness Good Times (3)

Rupert Markland decided to establish the actual level of interest in the Guinness Good Times product. To do this he commissioned a market research agency to carry out 250 street interviews in Dublin and 25 in-depth interviews of visitors from the UK and the US at Storehouse.

The results were excellent. Both the Guinness name and the beer went down well, and Markland obtained some good quotes to include in his management presentation. One-third of those interviewed believed that their trip could have been improved by buying 'insider' services such as guides and tours, while almost 90 per cent saw Guinness as the appropriate supplier with a unique competitive advantage. Finally, the research showed an indicative price of around between IRP 30 and 100. The annual revenue opportunity was small, however, at IRP 1 million.

Product feasibility

The uncertainty-reducing rule drives more expensive work in the product area into the Seed stage, but in Start the team has to do enough to convince the board of basic product feasibility. A prototype is useful in providing focus and in showing the venture review board that the idea is worthwhile. Diageo is not a travel company, so Rupert Markland chose to run two tours at an early stage in his venture to achieve both of these goals at low cost. The video archive team in Los Angeles, by contrast, fell in love with the technology behind its idea and spent all of its time and money developing a prototype.

Revenue model

A cogent proposal includes a revenue model showing how revenue is generated and collected. The heady days of flimsy dotcom models are long gone and a solid and credible model based on data from potential customers is the only way to convince a review board that the venture is valid.

We saw in GGT how Diageo included pricing questions in its Dublin survey. This approach works when end customers pay directly for the value delivered to them. Advertising and B2B models are trickier as the team has to ask end users a more complex set of questions about advertisement view rates and how they would pay channels.

Customer propensity to pay at various price levels (i.e. segmentation) is a key indicator of the acceptance of the business model. Only by using valid customer data can the team create a robust yet flexible model that allows it to vary its approach to different customer groups and maximize revenue. The team has to decide, for instance, whether it will use different price levels for different product combinations, perhaps delivering basic, intermediate and premium services (economy, business class and first class). Using this data, along with that established for market sizing, the team can generate initial revenue projections and start to size the whole business financially.

STRATEGIC THINKING

After marketing, the strategic qualities of the venture are its most important feature in Start. It is never too early to start thinking about which corporate assets the opportunity uses and extends. These assets also give the venture an advantage over existing and future competitors.

Using and extending assets

The job here is to understand the assets that the venture needs and then establish which of those the company possesses and will make available. Many ventures begin life with one product and one type of customer. The venture team can gain considerable credibility with management if it can demonstrate that the venture forms the basis of a major new business asset and is something around which the company can build other businesses. We refer to this in Chapter 11 as 'strategic importance'.

BAA, the airports management group, recognized in the late 1980s that it had a huge dormant asset in its UK airport terminals. By reusing unused space in the terminals as shopping malls, the company generated significant new revenues. Having perfected the approach and turned its assets into shopping malls with runways attached, the firm exported its expertise to other airports which had not developed the capability, such as Logan Airport in Massachusetts and Pittsburgh in Pennsylvania. Not only had an asset been reused to generate new revenue, but the knowledge and experience gained from the new business had also been crafted into a new facilities management venture.

Brand is an interesting asset. Roche Diagnostics disallows mention of the Roche brand as a relevant strategic asset by early-stage venture teams because it believes that a venture has to stand without it in the first instance. Guinness Good Times, on the other hand, became more about the brand as the venture evolved (see Example 9.4). The lesson here is again about 'subject think'. Just because the company contributes assets does not mean that the venture is viable. The opportunity has to exist and be profitable, regardless of the company, and only when it has been properly defined is it legitimate to consider the role that company assets might play.

Example 9.4   Guinness Good Times (4)

The original inspiration behind the Guinness Good Times venture was a desire by Guinness to apply its brands to other leisure activities and in passing create more brand loyalty. Rupert Markland had to show that the Guinness brand was appropriate for such a product and that there was little risk to it. So, he organized a series of brainstorming sessions with Guinness marketing executives to explore the relationship between his product concept and the brand. Although GGT has no plans to use its operations as a way of directly marketing

Guinness, the brainstorming sessions showed that a high-quality, upmarket Ireland travel product matched the Guinness brand statement and extended it safely into a new domain.

Advantages

Advantages come in two flavours – initial and sustainable. Initial advantages can include speed to market, access to existing customer channels, proprietary technology or the lack of existing competition. 'The group must look for an unfair advantage,' says Tim Forrest at Powergen. These 'unfair' advantages can often be taken directly from the host company at little or no cost.

When GM introduced OnStar in its Cadillac range it understood that it was alone in the automotive world in delivering such a system. As it had full access to the delivery mechanism for OnStar – GM produced over 2.5 million cars in 2000 – its initial advantage was substantial. It predicted that other manufacturers would soon obtain similar technology from other suppliers, but in the meantime it could involve and possibly retain a large number of GM owners and prospective buyers with this new product.

A sustainable competitive advantage is not easy to achieve. It typically arises from customer lock-in through a unique selling point such as a proprietary technology or employee expertise, a network effect, high switching costs, or a cost advantage that derives from economies of scale or of scope.

GETTING TO THE NEXT STAGE

Now comes the crucial test for the venture. Is it worth the company investing at least $300 000, and possibly 10 times as much, to work-up the idea to the point of major investment? For a company to consider the idea, answers to Batch 1 questions on the size of the revenue opportunity, the nature of the product and its customer, and what it has to do with the company, have to be clear and persuasive. Furthermore, the team has to make a series of reasonable, but unproven, claims about the Batch 2 marketing (channels, promotion, etc.) and product feasibility aspects of the venture (see Example 9.5).

Example 9.5 Guinness Good Times (5)

In January 2001, Rupert Markland made a presentation to the venture review board that oversaw his venture. On it sat Jim Grover (Group Strategy Director), Andrew Morgan (President of New Business Ventures) and Jon Potter (Guinness Global Brand Director).

He demonstrated a mock-up of the website. He then claimed that the annual margin potential was over IRP 1 million, and went on to mention two other important features of the business that made it more attractive to Diageo. The first was that other Diageo brands, such as Johnnie Walker and Smirnoff, could be the subjects of similar ventures. The second was that the concept could also be extended to the corporate travel market and marketed to companies as 'incentive travel' prizes on staff reward schemes.

These extensions grew the opportunity to over IRP 10 million. He then asked for £450 000 to take the business forward to product launch. Of this sum, £200 000 was for website development and the remainder was for further marketing development of the idea.

Most companies operate a 'star chamber' system such as the one used by Diageo, where the team goes to the company board room, often for the first time, and endures one or two hours of sudden death. The venture team needs to be well prepared with a presentation and a proposal document. Pre-meeting lobbying (which we describe in more detail in Chapter 12) helps the team to understand who is making the decisions and what is on their agenda.

A 3000-word mini business plan is usually enough to describe the venture, with the questions from Chapter 6 as headings. Venture unit staff standby to help, as this may be the first such piece of work for venture team members. A short budget and plan for the

Seed stage, and a 30-minute presentation, are enough to convey to senior executives the strategic and marketing essence of the business idea and further plans to develop the various other claims made.

Managing success and failure

The period after the review process can be tense as the team awaits a verdict on whether the company wants to back the idea or not. Either way, the venture unit's role is to congratulate the team for getting to the end of the Start stage and completing its tasks.

Four verdicts are possible: bad idea; good idea but more information needed; good idea but poor team; good idea. In the case of the first and third the venture unit has to manage the individuals whose venture dream is over. In the second, the Start stage continues until the venture unit judges that another request for funding is appropriate. If the review board supports the plan, the venture unit has to prevent team members immediately resigning their day jobs. This process needs gentle management, as resources can be jealously guarded and line managers want to know what it means in practice.

CONCLUSION

In this chapter we have made four major points about the Start stage:

- Start focuses on the opportunity itself (customer proposition and the product concept, and the scale of the revenue opportunity) and then its relevance to the firm.

- The venture team uses focus groups for the customer proposition and the product concept, and surveys for the revenue opportunity.

- The stage usually costs well under 1 per cent of the revenue opportunity, with research being the biggest expense.

■   The venture review board reviews a proposal, budget and presentation and considers the venture for Seed funding based on the team's answers to the six Batch 1 questions and claims made for Batch 2.

10 Seed

The Seed stage begins once the venture team has received finance to develop its idea and ends when the venture review board is convinced that the business is commercially viable. Tom Uhlman at Lucent New Ventures Group sums up this stage: 'We take research and researchers out of the labs – people who are working with an early stage project. Typically they have run out of standard lab-based funding and do not have a business unit looking to support the next stage. Usually there is just a technology and a concept at this stage. My team works with them, provides the commercial skills to help turn it into an embryonic business.'

During Seed, the team provides answers to all the questions we listed in Chapter 6, proving the claims made on Batch 2 questions in Start and also answering Batch 3 fully. Although product prototyping and perhaps some development may take place in order to enable detailed cost calculations for the financial plan, most of the work in Seed is market research. From this, answers to remaining strategy questions and the revenue side of the financial plan are derived. Mike Harris, who founded online financial supermarket Egg, says, 'I believe in customer immersion. We started from customer problems and needs and worked from there. We had a panel of 1000 people and talked to each face-to-face once a month for a year for our 'Year in the Life' qualitative research. Every week I sat in a focus group listening to what customers had to say.' At Diageo, too, market research dominated the Seed stage (Example 10.1).

Example 10.1   Guinness Good Times (6)

In January 2001, Rupert Markland's Guinness Good Times venture review board turned down his request for £450 000. The board felt that proceeding with expensive website development was unwise until marketing and product questions had been answered more fully.

Instead, the board gave Markland £100 000 to continue to develop and test the idea through the summer travel season until October 2001. In particular, he was told to work out a business model for GGT and to analyse a greater variety of marketing channels by which it could be sold. The board also insisted that he stick with Guinness, rather than broaden to other Diageo brands, and that he define and test the product better through a series of pilots for American visitors to Ireland. Rupert now says, 'I am glad about that. At the time it was something of a blow. But in retrospect the early work was incomplete. Had we gone ahead with development at that stage we would have risked wasting money and the project may well then have been discarded.'

Markland had been working alone, and decided he need some help with researching the market and organizing the pilot. He consulted the head of the New Business Ventures Incubation team, Raphael Offer (a former Coca-Cola marketing executive), and marketing executives in Guinness. Together, they found a Dublin-based marketing consultant to help Markland design and test packages in the summer. He also found a travel industry consultant in the US who was familiar with how the travel industry assembles and sells tour packages and who had good contacts. With this team, Markland set about filling in the gaps in his business plan.

The key lessons from GGT here are the balance between marketing and product development and the importance of a complete team. Marketing comes first in Seed on grounds of information 'bang for buck'. Revenue model and customer segmentation take over from customer proposition and product concept, which have by now been fully defined. The extent of product development is tricky, and depends on a couple of factors which we cover later in the chapter. The main extra outputs in this stage are the business and financial plans requesting investment, and the key is to keep planning, marketing and product in balance as this stage progresses.

In this chapter we look at how venture teams complete the marketing agenda we set out earlier with an emphasis on market research, product development, how to manage the venture team, and how to prepare for the Setup stage. We defer outstanding strategic questions to Chapter 11 as they form the basis of the investment decision.

FLEXIBILITY

Flexibility is essential in venture development if the benefits of the process are not to be lost in a mound of paper and unnecessary work. Consider the example of Arcus, a travel agency that in late 2000 seed-funded a project to develop a retail travel health service concept. The company's venture review board provided the team with sufficient funds for the whole Seed stage and suggested that it form a joint venture with a health company.

The manager of the venture unit thought that the project had too many unknowns for a credible budget to be possible. The customer proposition seemed sound but the product was impossible to deliver without a joint venture partner, and the team needed a marketing executive to carry out market research to gauge the take-up and pricing of the service. He decided to divide it into three stages with a venture unit review at the end of each of the first two.

The manager and the team agreed the three-stage split. The first stage target was the joint venture partner. The second was a team of four people to include one marketing professional. The third stage was the original plan agreed by the venture review board. The venture then proceeded on that basis.

As this example shows, Seed-stage projects are subject to some uncertainty about duration and cost. Too rigid a plan, and the venture team executes unnecessary tasks. Too loose a plan, and the team cuts information-generating work short and misses the one factor that will damage the business later. The solution is flexibility, and a good venture unit is ready at any stage, by agreement with the venture review board and the team, to:

- Alter the budget, the customer proposition or the product concept.

- Subdivide the Seed stage into mini-stages.

- Inject the venture into a joint venture with another firm.

- Accelerate or decelerate product development.

- Close the venture.

TEAM AND BUDGET

The venture unit takes the lead on team recruitment, the duration of the project and its budget. It negotiates the latter two with the team based on the stipulations of the venture review board and its own business judgement. Seed stage usually costs between 1 and 3 per cent of the revenue opportunity (less if there has been a Start stage), with the percentage driven mainly by the level of uncertainty inherent in the venture. The actual cost drivers are marketing and staff and product development, although attributed corporate services (especially legal) fees can play a part, as we shall see later with Guinness Good Times.

A reasonable minimum team size is three people, one for each of planning, marketing and product – exactly as Rupert Markland at Diageo found with his relatively small venture. The same person can do both planning and marketing if necessary, but few people have both sets of skills and such a team would be unbalanced and at risk of becoming product-led. There is no maximum, but more than 30 people is unusual. At Nokia, venture teams range in size from 5 to 60 people. Most teams are somewhere between 5 and 10 staff, with the level of product development being the determining factor.

Time is of the essence in venture development. Costs usually fall straight through to the firm's P & L, line managers want their staff back and senior managers want the plans yesterday at 7 a.m. Also some other enterprise is bound to be developing the same idea. All of this places a great deal of pressure on the venture team, of course, which the venture unit is there to reduce. Three months is a short time for the Seed stage, while a year is generally too long a time for a revenue opportunity below $500 million. The venture unit may also divide this period up into sub-stages for review and incentive purposes, as we saw in the Arcus example.

Team building

Successful venture teams are complete, balanced, motivated and skilled. 'Good teams can make bad projects scream, and bad teams can make fantastic projects implode', says Seth Samir at Schlumberger. Motivation is central to a venture's prospects. Although they may not have to express it formally, all team members need to make sure that they understand each other's motivations as they start out. If one member wants to be a millionaire and another just wants to save the world, the situation may not be compatible, and disruptive conflict may arise. Teams are much better served when all members understand where they all want to go.

This story of a venture team manager in a US manufacturing firm summarizes the HR issues facing the venture unit once Seed financing is granted.

> I came out of the room on a high. I knew we had got the money. The questioning was hostile and the CTO started going on about stuff I didn't understand. But the marketing guy and the head honcho were obviously on our side. Now I had a new job and was in control of my own destiny! For 6 months!
>
> Then Peter [the head of venturing] and I had a 2-hour meeting. I felt like I was signing away my life. The first thing he told me was that the

Business Venture Group had the right to stop the project any time. The next thing was I could be let go 3 months after it closed. Then I had to sign a form saying that I worked on the idea during company time and that I acknowledged that the statement in my contract of employment about intellectual property belonging to the company applied in this case. Suddenly I saw the risky half of risk and reward. So I asked him about rewards. He said they were working on it and told me some garbage about being paid bonuses if the business became profitable. Did I have a job if it got invested? Probably was the answer, we try to look after all the people who work with us but we can't guarantee it. When I left the meeting I went for a walk and thought about calling my former boss and asking her for my old job back.

The tasks for the venture unit and the entrepreneur, then, are to build a venture team, get the staff out of their old jobs, agree incentives, and deal with the IPR issue. These are whole lot more serious than in Start, as staff may be risking their careers on a venture.

Manager and executives

The venture unit will usually have to deal with the person who came up with the idea. It has a greater set of choices with people already working for the company than with those who have brought an idea to the company, and a common arrangement is to appoint the person Venture Manager in exchange for the loss of any IPR claim and control over the venture. But who does the Venture Manager report to? The venture unit's advisory and support role (in the flexible model from Chapter 7) suggests that a direct reporting relationship is not appropriate. Other choices are the head of the venture unit, a senior executive mentor from the venture review board, or nobody at all.

The rest of the venture team – venture executives – comes from a variety of places. 'There was a debate about how to staff the new programmes,' says Cliff Detz at ChevronTexaco, 'the initial approach was to use all newcomers and no existing personnel to avoid criticism of poaching and to inject new blood.' Under the flexible venture unit model (in use at GGT, where Rupert Markland filled out his team with staff outside Diageo's NBV group), staff come from elsewhere in the firm or from outside it altogether. Under the fixed model, they mostly come from the venture unit.

Staff transfer

Working in a venture team is risky because a venture can end at any point. This suggests that a formal arrangement between the venture unit and the venture team is needed. The other purpose of staff transfer terms is to allow venture team members to move from their old jobs and to feel secure in their positions in the firm while they build up the business. Moving people around is arduous, though. Tomas Ulin of Ericsson Business Innovation says, 'A huge part of my work is getting people in and out of the ventures. We do retain the right to move people. Sometimes this is difficult and we have to be creative. But we work to find new opportunities for those whose ventures are terminated.'

A formal arrangement can have its downsides. Rick Wills of British Airways never had to produce an HR deal for internal employees. He took the view that anybody scared of losing their BA position could 'leave Enterprises and go back to what they do best in the core business'.

This is a risky approach. There are two choices: new hire and secondment. New hire transfers the individual into a job underneath the venture unit and allows him to return to his old job if it is still available, whereas secondment keeps the old job open throughout. Powergen, for example, uses secondment for reasons of flexibility, reduced risk to the individual and less administrative hassle if the venture is terminated.

If the venture ends then the venture unit deals with company staff who have transferred rather than been seconded. The company should provide a lengthy period after the termination of the venture for the employee to find a new position. If the person finds no new job, then the company and the employee have to face the prospect of severance.

Incentives

Entrepreneurs have different risk–reward profiles. At one extreme, it is just another corporate job. At the other, the entrepreneurs want equity options and are prepared to leave the company and its benefits package behind. The offer to company staff is learning, training, independence and freedom. For companies, Seed-stage ventures are small, and it is not usually worth spending legal time at this stage on structuring for stock options or inventing a formula that pays out according to business value. Stock exchange rules in many countries require shareholders to be consulted before any such dilution of their asset.

Most firms use bonuses to provide incentives for internal staff. Bonuses are simple for the HR department to administer and easy for venture teams to understand. Powergen calculates a percentage of salary for the individual based on time spent on the project, personal performance and the project's success in attaining its targets. Roche Diagnostics uses the standard divisional system (a percentage of total compensation) to 'motivate people and encourage them to be entrepreneurial', while terms and conditions at Ericsson are the same in ventures as in the rest of the company. 'We don't want to create internal competition. Stealing people is bad,' says Tomas Ulin.

Intellectual property rights

For ventures that have come from outside, the IP resides in the joint venture struck between the entrepreneurs and the company. For internal ventures, the beginning of the Seed stage is the point where the IPR question is put to bed. The venture unit's bargaining position with internal staff is strong enough for it to demand an explicit acknowledgement of the company's IP rights. Tomas Ulin at Ericsson says, 'With internal ideas, there is no problem – the IPR belongs to Ericsson.'

MARKETING

Marketing is one of the two big activities within the Seed stage, costing up to 50 per cent of the overall costs of this stage, depending on the level of product development. By the time the Seed stage begins, a venture team has defined the customer proposition and the product concept and therefore has a clear idea of what the products will do and what customer activities they drive and support. It will also have an outline customer segmentation hypothesis, a brand hypothesis (where appropriate) and a sense from initial desk and market research of the revenue opportunity for each segment. Also, it will have some evidence of propensity to purchase.

Several marketing pitfalls await venture teams (and venture units) in the Seed stage. These disrupt ventures badly because financial planning and prototype development depend on marketing and mistakes there have a knock-on effect on the remainder of the project.

The first pitfall is undertaking full-scale quantitative market research before the customer proposition and product concept have been formulated and tested using qualitative research (see definitions below). Without these, the quantitative research is testing an incomplete set of hypotheses, may produce unreliable or incomplete data, and is likely to have to be redone. Next, there are many cases of venture teams confusing marketing consultancy with market research and expending their budget on expensive consultancy when all they wanted was research.

Market research agencies help with the logistics of testing hypotheses. Based on the hypotheses, the team defines the questions and works with the agency to define the number and nature of the targets, and the agency does the rest. Where the hypotheses (proposition, concept, segmentation) are incomplete, an agency may offer to help the team to complete them. This is marketing consultancy. It costs more and, like most consultancy, can get out of control when the buyer fails to define in advance the boundaries of the engagement.

A good venture unit is prepared for marketing work going awry and is ready to step in with advice and assistance. On occasions it is necessary to bring in a marketing advisor to lay out the land

and help the venture team plan a programme of research. The best source is the company itself. Failing that, an external specialist marketing consultant with experience in the industry is usually better than an advertising or market research agency, which may not be independent.

A sensible approach

Marketing, then, covers a wide range of tasks, whose outputs feed into the business and financial plans. The goals are to form for each segment a marketing strategy (revenue model, pricing, competitive differentiation, channels, promotion and branding), define the products in detail and produce a revenues forecast for the financial plan. Virtually all of the work involves generating hypotheses and then testing them through research.

Example 10.2   Guinness Good Times (7)

Guinness Good Times Venture Manager Rupert Markland wrestled with segmentation, business and revenue model and product definition questions. Should events be combined into groups and sold as a package, or should they be sold individually? What packages of events made sense? Furthermore, what type of people could they be sold to and for how much? Who precisely would deliver these products on the ground in Ireland?

Given that Diageo was not going to get directly involved in operating tours, there were three options for GGT's business model. One was the joint venture, where Diageo and one or more travel industry partners would create a new company and each inject assets, people and money to start the business. The second was a franchise system, under which Diageo would define the products and then licence them and the brand to tour operators who would be responsible for operating and marketing them. The last was a product and licensing model, where the brand would be licensed to operators for use in tours to be devised, produced and marketed by them according to the licence conditions.

Markland and his colleagues quickly dismissed the franchise option because it required Diageo to be involved in product definition long term, something that they felt required a continuing competence in travel. Franchising also suggested competing tour operators, whereas the Guinness brand demanded uniqueness. Of the other two, the joint venture option too required Diageo to maintain travel industry expertise over the long term, albeit only non-executive. It also required a larger initial financial commitment and locked-in the business risk of disputes with the joint venture partner at a later date. On the other hand, the licensing model's only disadvantage was that it was potentially difficult to retain control over the use of the Guinness brand (although this was later solved). With this in mind, Markland consulted his board and reached agreement that licensing was the way to go.

The first and most important task, then, is to complete hypotheses for segmentation and, for each segment, a revenue model and an outline product definition from qualitative research using focus groups. These feed into quantitative research to assess customer numbers and pricing and to test the hypotheses. Venture marketing is an iterative process with new information arriving continuously and prototype development quite possibly happening at the same time. It is a tough proposition for many venture teams, even those with a marketing specialist in their ranks. In Guinness Good Times, for example, this research involved a change in business model (see Example 10.2).

Structuring research

The trick in market research is to work out at the beginning what questions need answering, the definition of the target group, and the research method. There are two research methods – qualitative and quantitative. Qualitative is a dialogue-based method useful for forming hypotheses about what the product should do, who the customers might be, their segmentation and so on. The main qualitative technique, as we have seen, is focus groups.

Quantitative is a question-and-answer method, usually involving questionnaires, useful for testing and proving hypotheses once they have been formed by qualitative means.

Qualitative almost always comes before quantitative. In fact, much of the qualitative work will have been done before the Seed stage starts, although quantitative work may show that some of the hypotheses are unsound. In this case the qualitative work needs to be redone. Quantitative research, by contrast, is where the venture team spends its Seed marketing budget to prove hypotheses about segmentation, product definition, et cetera. Winning investment depends heavily on the team answering questions about customer numbers and revenue model. Table 10.1 lists the functions of a quantitative research programme.

Unless the proposed product is a specialized B2B product with a small potential market, venture teams do not usually go out and interrogate potential customers directly. Market research agencies have the manpower and databases to do that and are more efficient. The venture team's task is to establish the hypotheses and then work out the questions, the target group definition and the research method. Once these are done, the team can commission a market research agency to do the rest, taking care to use the agency only for research.

Table 10.1 Functions of quantitative research

Element	Goal
Segmentation	Prove the market segmentation is valid.
Value and price	Establish how much the revenue collection model will generate per customer.
Revenue model	Prove that the revenue collection method will work.
Positioning	Prove that the products occupy their designated slot in the product hierarchy.
Promotion	Prove that branding and promotion strategies will work.
Customer numbers	Forecast customer numbers.

PRODUCT

The overall job in product during the Seed stage is to assess all the elements necessary for development, operation and support of the product once investment has been received. These together constitute the product logistics, which in turn drive the cost model in the financial plan. As with revenues, small shifts in parameter values are enough to tip a positive NPV heavily negative.

Example 10.3   Guinness Good Times (8)

The licensing decision altered the nature of Diageo's Guinness Good Times proposition. The tour operators had to be capable of devising new products as well as operating them, and GGT was now cast as a company licensing the Guinness brand to the travel industry rather than as a travel industry company in its own right.

The marketing consultant and Markland brainstormed a long list of possible Guinness-related events and used six-person focus groups to match individual events to wealth- and age-group combinations. After a series of iterations, they ended up with a set of events that corresponded to age groups in the upper echelon professionals segment, all of them 'differentiated and unique, premium and quality'. The list included Gaelic games, walks, genealogy and barge trips, while the original pub tour fell away. Storehouse became the venue for literary, culinary and music activities. During the summer, GGT found service providers and piloted six of these events in Dublin. The team received customer feedback on the events and the service providers.

At the end of 2001, Markland and the travel consultant launched a programme to select five US-based tour operators. The consultant introduced Markland to nine of these, and together they devised evaluation criteria which included Ireland travel volume, quality, trustworthiness and creativity. After a series of interviews and due diligence, they selected five. The commercial arrangement with each of them was that Diageo would receive a percentage of the total package price excluding airfares. At the same time, Markland contacted Diageo's legal department for help with the licensing contract.

The relevant product activities vary enormously by venture type. Rupert Markland's experiences with Guinness Good Times are typical of what is expected in the Seed stage (see Example 10.3). More generically, the venture team would expect to cover the following:

■ Develop product, prototype or design, perhaps including technology.

■ Determine whether product inputs will be created by venture, supplied by contracted suppliers or by partners.

■ Secure supply of product inputs and design production process.

■ Establish customer support model.

■ Establish service model (maintenance, repair and improvement).

How much development

The biggest issue in product during the Seed stage is the level of development. Because they are keen to show that their product is feasible, and the company is also keen to know, venture teams frequently favour development at the expense of marketing. We saw this earlier with GGT and its software development plan which was, wisely, turned down by the Diageo NBV board. The venture unit's task is to keep development down to what is useful and prevent the team from running away with the product. It has therefore to help the team make a strategic decision about how far development should go.

The venture team has three choices for product development during the Seed stage. In descending order of expense they are:

- To fully develop the product.

- To design the product, build a prototype and perform a feasibility review.

- To design the product and perform a feasibility review.

Let us return to the uncertainty-reducing logic we defined in Chapter 6. While higher levels of development inevitably cost more, they also serve to reduce the level of uncertainty around the product. Depending on the product in question, the reduction of uncertainty is critical as it establishes the feasibility of the product, increases the reliability of market forecasts and communicates the seriousness of the project to industry participants.

How does one choose the appropriate level of expenditure on development? That depends on the nature of the relationship between cost and uncertainty. Figure 10.1 represents these on a map of cost versus uncertainty. We can identify three scenarios:

- Where the cost of development is low and the uncertainty around the product is high, it is worth pushing for a full development of the product. For example, the Guinness Good Times concept was inexpensive, so it was fully developed as a way of establishing its viability. Aon's Unclaimed Asset Register (see Chapter 12) was also in this category.

- Where the cost of development is high and the uncertainty around the product is low, it is appropriate only to design the product and perform feasibility within the Seed stage and await further rounds of funding. For example, BG Group pursued a mobile telecoms venture (see below) which was expensive to implement but conceptually quite straightforward, so the Seed stage consisted of little more than design.

- Where the cost of development is in balance with the level of uncertainty around the product, the best bet is to build a prototype. Prototyping allows the venture team to identify and resolve the major uncertainties without incurring the

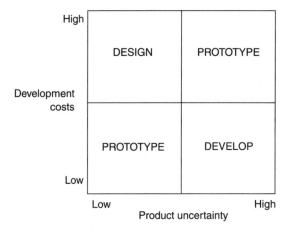

Figure 10.1   Seed product development: uncertainty versus cost

full costs of development. Many software development projects fit into this category.

Joint venture

As development work unfolds, the venture team develops sources for all the inputs and the processes needed for production. For all of these, the venture team has three basic choices: it can purchase the input from a supplier, it can license the right to produce the input, or it can partner with the supplier in some form of joint venture.

The decision to partner is made for a number of reasons. Sometimes it is to share the risk in a venture; sometimes it is because the active involvement of the partner is better achieved by giving it an ownership stake; and sometimes the supplier in question simply demands a partnership arrangement.

Consider the case of Spectrasite Transco. Until 2000, when it was floated as part of Lattice Group, Transco was the division responsible for physical distribution of gas by BG Group. For some time the idea had floated around Transco that its sites, such as gasholders and pressure reduction stations, could host network equipment for mobile telecommunications firms. In late 1999, it decided to form a business to exploit these geographically dispersed assets.

Andy Morrison took on the Venture Manager role and formed a venture team consisting of telecommunications and real estate consultants (Transco's experience of both industries was thin), and staff from Transco's regulatory and strategy functions. The team researched the industry and found that making sites available was only half the product story. Towers had to be designed and built to handle equipment from multiple mobile firms. Getting planning permission for these towers and building and maintaining them all required skills and experience. Moreover, a small cadre of specialist firms intermediated between site owners on one side, and mobile firms on the other, managing the sites and acting as consolidators.

The team realized that Transco alone could not process sites fast enough or develop the skills needed to build towers and manage the sites themselves. Nor could it be its own consolidator. The team decided to seek a joint venture partner from among the specialist consolidators. It chose Spectrasite, and Spectrasite Transco was born in summer 2000 in a joint venture valued at £140 million.

In this case, Transco found that other firms owned key assets and that it couldn't develop them itself. It therefore faced a choice between continuing to develop its business independently to improve its bargaining position, to try to get a firm to act as a supplier, or to solicit a deal. Because the intermediary firms managed the relationship with the mobile firms as well as looking after the sites, Transco could not reasonably expect an intermediary firm to become a supplier, and it chose to do the deal.

Access to help

The venture unit helps to secure assistance with legal issues from the company or from an outside law firm (see Example 10.4) and with strategic financial issues from corporate finance. The venture team is almost bound to be inexperienced in both of these fields, and the costs of blundering are high.

Example 10.4   Guinness Good Times (9)

In January 2002 Markland was able to demonstrate conclusive progress on all fronts. He put together a financial plan for 2002 that showed a total negative cash-flow of £150 000 and returned to his venture review board with a request for that sum. For that investment, he promised to negotiate the license fees and wrap up the legal arrangements with the operators in Ireland and the travel tour operators in the US, to formulate a marketing plan, and then to launch the business in the summer of 2002 with a total of 60 events.

Not having worked on legal issues before, Markland ran into three difficulties. Firstly, the legal department was fully occupied with an acquisition. The second was the scale of the effort required to produce an original contract which, among other things, protected both the GGT business and the Guinness brand against every possible contingency. The third was that each line item in the contract had to work for the five counter-parties, and negotiating these took time and effort.

With the help of an outside law firm, Markland worked through these problems. The result was a 50-page 'Irish Travel Series Presented By Guinness' licensing contract. Now the principal asset of GGT, the five signed contracts ensured that Diageo retained all Intellectual Property Rights in the events and had the right of approval for new events and marketing materials. They also placed liability firmly in the hands of the operators. For each individual trip Diageo is to receive between 10 and 18 per cent of the cost less airfares, equating to between $100 and $300 per person – substantially higher than expected in the original business case 18 months earlier.

Corporate services groups are often stretched and access to them can be difficult. The senior executives on the venture review board can assist in clearing obstacles out of the way and getting the venture team the help it needs.

PREPARING FOR SET-UP

As the Seed stage nears completion, the venture starts to look less like a group of researchers and more like a business unit in the making. Although venture team staff are primarily concerned about getting investment, their thoughts also turn to the management of the business, their own futures and what level of risk and reward they are looking for. The venture unit's job is to stop managing the venture, get it out of the business creation process and set it up as a freestanding entity correctly positioned inside, or outside, the company with a management team, remuneration and incentives, agreed deliverables, and so on. In doing so, the unit's role mutates from doctor, professor and engineer to non-executive director.

The length and complexity of this process means that an early start is necessary. Firstly, the unit has to determine the chances of the venture receiving investment funding and then deal with longer-lead items such as its capital structure and management recruitment. Next, during the 'No Man's Land' period waiting for investment, the venture unit has to manage the team, find bridging finance if necessary, and keep the venture moving.

Manage the team

Managing the team involves maintaining morale while it waits for investment financing. Teams can be hyped up and used to working all hours, and suddenly having nothing to do can be trying. Some members may be tempted to look for another job within the firm or even go back to their old jobs, and consultants on a promise of a job should investment arrive may also start to look for their next project. At the same time, a good venture unit prepares the team for a possible failure to secure investment and encourages members to line-up other work while reminding them of the employment deal.

Expand the team

It is never too early to start work on hiring the management team. The unit and the venture team between them define all the management job positions. The unit works-up job descriptions and a recruitment strategy for each and decides which venture team members, if any, go into these positions. Reconciling these with the ambitions and hopes of members of the venture team in place for the Seed stage becomes essential at this point.

Keep moving

The best solution for venture team frustration while waiting for investment is a holiday followed by planning and design work if a decision has still not been reached. Many venture teams preparing business and financial plans to a deadline neglect to plan the detail of what will happen the day after investment is secured. Work on detailed product designs and project plans for product development and market rollout is an excellent use of the team's time and a good introduction for any new staff. Continued demonstration to potential customers helps line-up sales, and legal work on customer contracts gets the business ready to execute once investment arrives.

Begin the separation

Fax machines and office telephones do not grow on trees. When a venture emerges from the Seed stage it may find that independence removes many of the free benefits that it had previously enjoyed, such as office space and equipment, professional services such as legal counsel and HR, technical and development costs, right through to coffee and water machines. The team has to act independently and negotiate terms for all these services at arm's length, while always looking to maximize unfair advantage.

Each member of the team took a risk by becoming involved in the venture. Now the risk becomes real. If the venture is spun-out, each team member will have to resign from the parent company and sacrifice the benefits that it provided. These typically include healthcare, pension arrangements, vacation entitlements and many others. With luck, team members will already have weaned themselves off such benefits, but the break is real and needs to be addressed. If spun-in, these issues are less pressing, as terms and conditions often remain the same or similar. In both cases, the individual's corporate life has now gone forever.

CONCLUSION

In this chapter we have made seven major points about the Seed stage:

■ Flexibility is essential. The venture unit has to be ready to alter any aspect of the venture and to shut it at any time.

■ Venture teams are full-time. Internal staff must be transferred from their old jobs.

■ Before the Seed stage begins, teams working on internal ideas must relinquish any IPR claim.

■ If either of the product concept or the customer proposition is incomplete then the venture must return to the Start stage.

■ Marketing work is mostly quantitative research to test hypotheses about revenue model, product definition, and segmentations.

■ Venture teams should prototype, or design, rather than develop products, unless development reduces uncertainty cost-effectively.

■ The venture unit manages the process throughout, especially at the end when the venture team is awaiting investment.

11 Set-up

As a child grows older its relationship with its parents undergoes steady change. After the years of innocence come the rebellious years of adolescence, followed by an increasing lust for financial and decision-making independence – subjects at school, choices of friends and evening activities. What are the parents to do? Ignore, fight, or grudgingly accept the changes, or facilitate them in the hope that a new relationship will be born?

So it is when a venture has received investment finance. The need to complete the new business and position it inside or outside the firm becomes urgent. Does the parent company jealously guard its progeny and do its best to pay management according to the old pocket money salary scale? Or does it develop a relationship that maximizes value on the basis of sound strategic reasoning? Rob Kirschbaum of DSM describes the latter course as the 'freedom to claim value'.

Set-up is the last stage in the business creation process, beginning when an investment decision about the venture is made and ending when the business can manage its operations independently of the venture unit. Set-up is about leaving the protective embrace of the parent company and learning how to be independent. By this time customers may be signed up, supplier contracts activated, production systems ready to go live and new employees about to start. This is an exciting time for the team as its dream finally becomes real and the hard work of planning begins to bear fruit.

FUNDING AND POSITIONING

The parent company has five options for the new venture. The venture can be spun-in as a 100 per cent-owned business unit or as a majority-owned subsidiary, or it can be spun-out as a joint venture or as a minority-owned company. Lastly, it can be sold outright or shut (see Table 11.1).

Choosing the ownership model

By the time a venture is ready to go all questions in the marketing, product and organization and risk categories have been dealt with satisfactorily. The parent company now looks at strategic and financial potential. We have defined these at length in previous chapters, and at the point of investment they boil down to:

■ *Strategic fit* – the proportion of necessary assets that the parent possesses.

■ *Financial attractiveness* – the scale of the financial opportunity.

■ *Strategic importance* – the value of the new assets the venture is creating.

Table 11.1   Ownership options at investment

Option	Form	Investment structure
Spin-in	Business unit	Parent (100%)
Spin-in	Subsidiary	Parent (90–100%) and staff (10–0%)
Spin-out	Joint Venture	Parent (30–70%), other companies (70–30%), staff (rest)
Spin-out	Investment offering	Parent (<50%), other companies, venture capital firms and staff (>50%)
Out	Sale or closure	Anybody – venture capital firms, companies, staff

The first two of these criteria are the axes of our business development model (Fig. 2.3). Just as this model is instrumental in choosing ideas to develop using business creation, so it is instrumental in deciding which ventures to fund and own. 'Strategic fit' is another term for initial competitive advantage ('unfair advantage' in Tim Forrest's words), and some companies, such as Shell, add a corroboration test for strategic fit – whether an internal division is prepared to fund the venture – as a market test of that criterion.

To these two familiar criteria we now add a third. The strategic importance of any new assets the business may be creating is a measure of its option value, and makes up for lower financial attractiveness. Let us look at a few examples to see the interplay of these three factors.

Consider Tesco.com, the online sales arm of Tesco. Clearly, Tesco had most of the marketing and product logistical assets it needed to make this new venture happen. The financial scale of the opportunity was also substantial. Why did Tesco decide to keep Tesco.com an in-house venture rather than set up a joint venture with someone who could do the deliveries and operate the IT? What tipped the balance was the strategic importance of the venture to Tesco and the relative lack of importance of these new assets versus those that Tesco already possessed. In other words, strategic fit and strategic importance. For Tesco, there was nothing to be gained by bringing in an asset-wielding strategic investor. A financial investor perhaps, but for such a core proposition? – no way. So, Tesco.com is firmly part of Tesco, and that's the way we expect it to stay.

Mondex, on the other hand, was a stored-value card business designed in the early 1990s by the UK's National Westminster Bank. It was expected to replace cash for somewhere between 20 and 40 per cent of transactions by offering security as well as replicating the portability and ease of use of cash. This venture was one of the boldest by any large firm in the 1990s and threatened to move a central function of the banking system – clearing and cash management – to a new business model. After several years of gestation the venture was officially launched by National Wesminster as a combination of franchise and investment offering. Banking was, and still is, a territorial business, and the co-operation of at least one bank in each territory was needed in order to roll Mondex out. The aim was that a single consortium of banks in each territory would license the Mondex name and technology and then deploy it across its territory. Tim Jones, who conceived the idea and developed it for a decade, says, 'Someone had to go to the reserve bank in each jurisdiction and clear it with them. There was no way we could do that the world over.'

This decision must have been a difficult and controversial one for the bank. The venture met our second criterion, scale, easily enough – the product wasn't called 'Mondex' for nothing. National Westminster had all the assets it required to roll out the product bar regulatory relationships. But, what of the strategic importance of the new asset? This was everything and nothing, in our view. Everything because Mondex was a disruptive technology that may have tipped retail banks into a scramble in which NatWest had an advantage. Nothing because other banks with their regulatory access effectively controlled global roll-out. However, had National Westminster limited its roll-out to the UK only, then it would have satisfied all three of our criteria, so that keeping the venture in-house would have been the right course of action.

GM chose to keep OnStar, a car-based platform for mobile communications that we featured in Chapter 9, to itself as it started up, even though the OnStar venture team proposed to market it to other automobile makers. This approach fulfils our third criterion, strategic importance. GM sells cars, and OnStar's first job is to sell more of them and produce a competitive advantage. The profitability of the venture, while important, comes second to this strategic mission.

Diageo used this reasoning for its travel venture, Guinness Good Times. Early on in the venture, when Rupert Markland envisaged that GGT would itself market and operate the Ireland tours, our criteria would have suggested a joint venture with a large tour operator. However, strategic fit ruled this option out – there was to be no reduction of Diageo's total control over the Guinness brand. The part of the venture that owned the rights to use the Guinness name had to be wholly owned. So, Markland has since turned the venture into a brand licensor, and Diageo will keep 100 per cent of it.

Problems with business unit

Spinning-in covers two options: a wholly owned business unit and a majority-owned arms-length subsidiary. However, spinning a loss-making venture back into the company as a business unit rarely works. Take the example of Mike Grant, CEO of Secant Energy, a gas pipeline-based venture which had been set up within a division of Decadia (see Example 11.1). Grant quickly realized that his boss had little understanding of Secant and was unsympathetic to its need for special attention. When his boss was replaced, all Grant's suggestions about changing Secant's sales model were scotched. The problem was that Secant Energy was a misfit within its division, and this ended up killing the business.

Example 11.1   Set-up challenges at Decadia

After a year of venture development ending in December 1998, Secant Energy was set up as a business unit within a division of international conglomerate Decadia. Secant had recently completed hiring management and was racing ahead with infrastructure development and an early awareness marketing campaign. Secant's CEO, Mike Grant, reported to the divisional head.

Shortly after Grant started the problems began. In June 1999 the divisional financial projections showed a $10 million shortfall in its 1999 projected contribution of $125 million. In order to get back on track, cost cuts were necessary. $2 million of the $8 million loss budgeted in 1999 for Secant was lopped off. Suddenly, the business plan on which Secant had been funded had to be rewritten before any revenues had even been earned.

While dealing with this, Mike Grant found that his boss had little time to spend on the new venture. Secant was the smallest by far of the nine business units reporting into him, so he had decided to deal with Secant only when forced. This spelled disaster for Grant, who needed to get approval for a significant change in the business plan. As well as selling infrastructure access through intermediaries, Grant's new marketing director wanted to hire a direct sales force to get the business going with a bang. This required an extra $2 million investment on top of the $30 million agreed back in 1998, a $750 000 increase in the loss for 1999, and associated changes to the incentive plan.

Just when Grant had managed to get this on to his boss' agenda, the boss moved to a new job and a new person started. Soon after that the division began a review of Secant's operations and business plan. The result was a 'no' to the sales force request and a further cut in the 1999 loss of $1.5 million. Grant resigned from Decadia in November 1999 and Secant Energy was dead by January 2000.

A BG venture unit executive had a similar experience once the ventures he had started were put into a division. The executive found that the division's internal reporting processes, which were appropriately rigorous for a large operating business, were not suitable for new ventures. 'This was a planning operation which took a mechanical view of the businesses. We needed to be able to change our plans now and again, which didn't fit the model. The various types of targets – utilization, efficiency, etc. – that Finance used were irrelevant. They wanted to be able to compare and benchmark business units. Ours were outside this system. It just didn't work.'

Other executives have a similar view. 'There was loads of NIH [not invented here] and often it was too much to take on for unsure revenue flows,' says one of the executives involved in Belleron's venturing activities (see Chapter 4). Roche Diagnostics finds that handing a venture over to a business unit too early can lead to difficulties and prefers to keep it in the venture unit for the full course.

We can see the internal tensions that make it difficult for new ventures to sit inside the operating divisions of large companies in *Focused* mode. These are:

■ A P & L-focused operating division is financially incompatible with a loss-making start-up business.

■ The substantial non-executive attention required by a new business cannot usually be provided by divisional management.

■ New business remuneration systems are incompatible with their divisional equivalents.

■ Divisions cannot give start-ups the stable funding background that they need while they execute their business plan.

■ Divisional measurement systems are incompatible with the targets usually set new ventures.

An *Integrated* company has, by definition, solved these problems and dispersed business creation throughout its divisions. We deal with this in Chapter 14.

Spinning-in

How does the parent company deal with the business when it emerges from the business creation process? Business units appear not to work. This leaves the option of forming an arms-length subsidiary, or of delaying the finding of a final home for the new business until more is known about it.

Ericsson places newly-hatched ventures in an independent receiving unit within the core of the company. The ventures stay there, financed separately to cash flow positive, until they find a home within the company. The other is an arms-length subsidiary. With this format, the parent:

■ Provides the venture with a higher level of independence from changes in the parent while keeping it in close contact with the group.

■   Sets up a board to manage the business more closely than a single line executive can.

■   Separates the business financially, thereby providing a stable funding background.

■   Avoids policy and process clashes between the new venture and older business units within the firm.

■   Is free to alter the status of the business if it remains 100 per cent owned.

It is usually simpler to constitute the venture as a subsidiary at the outset rather than disentangle its assets from the parent at a later stage if it becomes necessary for a flotation, sale or joint venture. With its own budget and reporting structure, the venture can operate relatively freely while retaining access to its source of unfair advantage.

This form of spin-in seems to be the most successful because by creating this type of vehicle the company sends a clear message to the team. There are myriad examples of successful businesses, formed from ventures, which started out as wholly-owned subsidiaries, including Prudential's Egg, Midland Bank's Direct Line and General Motors' Onstar.

The final question with spinning-in is whether the parent should retain full control over the business. The strongest reason for moving-off 100 per cent is to provide stock options to management and staff and hence to give them the assurance of independence. Such a move comes at the cost of total control. By law in most jurisdictions, directors have to be appointed and to take the interests of minority shareholders into account. The parent company would have to buy the minorities out if it decided to reintegrate the venture into its line management structure later on. This is complicated, expensive, unpredictable and ultimately unnecessary (see later in this chapter) if the parent company uses bonuses instead of equity.

Spinning-out

Spinning a venture out makes sense under either of the following circumstances:

- Access to external assets significantly increases the chances of successful execution.

- The venture is not of sufficient strategic importance and the firm does not consider financial attractiveness alone to be a valid reason to subscribe the total investment itself.

If the first criterion is met, then a joint venture is appropriate. Otherwise, an investment offering is the better solution. Spinning-out, though, is a complex process. Other companies become involved, as do lawyers. For the parent company, a spin-out mitigates its risk but also prevents it from subsequently pursuing other attractive businesses that emerge from the venture's activities. For the venture this choice enables it to gain access to other assets and perspectives on the business free from the parent company.

Joint venture

A joint venture is suitable when the venture requires significant assets which other companies possess. Most problems with joint ventures come from disagreement over strategy and level of control by the parents. As Portisco found out with its joint venture Accordant (described in Chapter 6), finding the right partner and the right reasons to go into a venture together is hard. In this case the decision was made too early and presupposed the outcome before sufficient research had been performed.

Investment offering

If the company wishes to stay involved, but does not want to retain majority ownership, it can sell the majority of the business. The team may have found potential investors in the business as it developed the concept during the Seed stage. However, if there are no obvious investors then the venture can search for venture capital funding. If the size of the investment is small the team might want to see if it can create a 'friends and family' investment fund.

Disposal

If the parent decides that the venture has merit but is no longer appropriate for its portfolio, it may decide to sell it. The sale of such an embryonic unit may not be simple, especially if it uses significant parental assets which are not for sale, such as brand.

Investment limits

Our research highlights a paradox that affects the way some firms look at the decision of funding and positioning a new business.

Consider the case of Pentameter Inc., a US chemicals company headquartered in the Midwest. In 1999, a venture team spent 6 months of its spare time, and some unofficial work time, producing a business plan to set up a subsidiary, code-named Tintagel, to market a new product to both existing and new customers. The idea was based on a process improvement which cut the cost of producing the new product by 50 per cent, giving it an economic advantage over substitutes. The team had filed for three patents and reckoned the total investment at $26 million with break-even in 3 years.

The Tintagel plan was passed up to Pentameter's CFO for a final decision. After an agonisingly long delay the team was told 'no'. A CEO review confirmed the decision. The team requested a meeting with both executives to discuss the proposal, and was given half an hour. At the meeting the executives conceded that nothing was wrong with the proposal. Its IRR and payback period were within acceptable thresholds, and this was a suitable venture for Pentameter that opened up a strategic bridgehead into the new market that the team identified. However, the funding requirement for the first 3 years would reduce the firm's earnings by an unacceptable amount. What, the executives asked, would happen if the precedent were set and other such ventures arrived? Pretty soon there would be no earnings left. There was no way it could be done.

The Tintagel team had expected this and asked for permission to approach another chemicals firm, with which Pentameter had a good relationship, with a proposal for a joint venture. To which the response was, 'Certainly not. This venture is too close to home to share. We would want all the value from this for ourselves.'

How does one make sense of this? The executives here were using an earnings argument against doing the venture in-house and a strategic or value argument against sharing it with another firm. This is another business creation paradox, and we define it in this way:

> Simultaneously not engaging a strategic partner for reasons of strategic importance or financial attractiveness while also not funding the business because of the dictates of managing for earnings.

When this paradox strikes, good business opportunities fall by the wayside. Why? Because executives in large quoted firms can run up against an investment limit set by the availability to them of investment capital and the need to maximize earnings in the short term. The solution, which we outline in the last chapter, is to separate the financial management and reporting of operating and investment businesses and to communicate separately about each to the stock market. This allows the market to place a separate value on the firm's earnings businesses and its growth businesses, and insulates the firm from shifts in the market's sentiment between the two types of business.

SETTING UP A SUBSIDIARY

In this final section on the mechanics of turning ideas into businesses we briefly explain how to set up a subsidiary. This is mostly the work of lawyers, but there are some business issues. We go through these in turn. First, the team – hiring and transferring it.

Next, remuneration and incentives. We then finish with the question of the relationship with the parent company.

Team

At the investment stage there may well be a substantial personnel changeover. Many people who like to work at the beginning of a venture may not want to carry on doing so once it has become established. Moreover, an invested venture needs a proper management team, unlike one in the Start or Seed stages.

There are three initial points to consider in this regard. First, management takes time to hire, and a good early start is necessary. Headhunters can usually be bargained down to a lower fee in the event that the venture does not obtain funding in exchange for a higher fee in the event that the hire is made. Second, if the founding idea owner (if there is one) is not going to be offered a management job in the venture, the venture unit's job is to find him or her something else to do. This can be tricky as treatment perceived to be unfair may affect the perception of the venture unit within the firm. A compromise based on the entrepreneur's needs usually works. Third, it may make sense to hire services people such as legal and human resources staff into the venture at this stage rather than rely on the parent company to continue to assist.

The main job, however, is venture team transfer. The big question that internal venture team members ask at this point is, 'Do the terms of my employment change if I take part in the venture?' The answer depends on whether staff have to change employer and on employment law within the jurisdiction concerned. A new company is formed for all but the 100 per cent-owned spin-in format. This new company may have different terms and conditions of employment from the parent and team members. If so, transfer of staff to the new vehicle may be affected by legislation, even if that transfer is made voluntarily. Lonnie Shoff at Roche Diagnostics emphasizes the importance of this issue: 'In the last stage of the venture process we have to create a unique HR contract for each person. Each country has its own laws and we can't produce a single policy. This is not easy.'

Incentives and remuneration

Throughout the venture development process the venture unit manages remuneration and incentives. While important in attracting and retaining team members throughout the life of the venture, the issue can become contentious as the business develops, especially if it begins to be successful. Rewards are established for future, rather than past, performance and work best when aligned to value created. But how can one measure value in a 100 per cent-owned subsidiary in the absence of a liquidity event such as a sale or flotation? Many companies have struggled with the question of risk and reward in venture development. One school of thought maintains that high risk–reward (venture teams leave the firm in exchange for stock options) works best, while the other (majority) school maintains that well-targeted bonuses avoid unnecessary cost and complexity.

Four options over and above straight salary each have their advantages and disadvantages in terms of flexibility, simplicity, cost, control (i.e. whether the parent cedes total control over the venture) and alignment of incentives with the value created in the venture. Table 11.2 rates these four options against these five criteria from the parent company's point of view.

Table 11.2   Venture remuneration options

Method	Flexibility	Simplicity and ease of use	Cost	Control	Alignment
Bonuses	Good	Good	Good	Good	Poor
Options in the venture	Poor	Medium	Poor	Poor	Good
Options in the parent	Poor	Good	Medium	Good	Poor
Phantom options	Poor	Poor	Poor	Good	Good

Bonuses

This is the simplest and most flexible option. It costs the parent and the venture little, and doesn't involve the parent ceding control over the venture. However, its alignment is poor. Many firms use bonuses because they score four 'Good's out of five.

Bonuses can work in a variety of ways. Take NorthStar Internet-working, an Internet service testing venture started in 1998 within Teradyne, the Boston-based testing and diagnostics firm. NorthStar was founded by MIT graduates Hollie and Peter Schmidt and set up as an arms-length unit within Teradyne with funding from the company's Telecoms Test Division.

The staff at NorthStar were excited by the possibility of a lucrative IPO, but a compensation plan had to be devised for executives that would reward their efforts while still acknowledging that they were part of Teradyne. So NorthStar adopted the divisional plan, which comprised a mix of salary (two-thirds of maximum total compensation), and a variable element (one-third) which depended on the performance of Teradyne (one-sixth) and the operating division to which NorthStar reported (one-sixth). As Peter and Hollie observed, staff were also motivated by the possible IPO: 'the idea that they were at the front of the line when the feast begins'.

In terms of the bonuses for venture unit managers, some use a formal 'carried interest' model that gives them a share of the equity in their portfolio companies. More commonly they receive a capped bonus based on long-term performance. One venture unit manager says 'We have developed a compromise that includes a base salary that follows the company norm. Then a bonus system which is kind of carried interest, in that it is based on EBIT for the venture. This is capped but at a very high level so that in a good year we can get up to board-level rewards. The money is vested over 3 years so there is always an incentive to stick around.'

Options in the parent

These are useful for aligning the interests of the venture management team with those of the parent company, if that is desired. Otherwise, they are a waste of time because bonuses outperform or equal them in every category.

Options in the venture

These were the lifeblood of the dotcom era but suffered later. They are more complex, cost more to design and manage, and are less flexible than bonuses. Granting too few to any individual may provide an insufficient incentive and does not encourage outstanding performance. Too many and the company runs the risk of employees becoming complacent – 'why sweat when I'm a millionaire?'

This method also suffers because of its effect on the parent's P & L and because of its dilution of parent company control. The P & L effect arises because when stock options are awarded the firm must (in most jurisdictions) account for them in that accounting period, whereas the increase in business value attained by the venture can only be recognized in the P & L much later, when (and if) a liquidity event occurs. The stock option P & L losses at the beginning should be negated later, because if there is no increase in value there should be no loss. However, that doesn't stop the P & L falling in the short term.

This P & L effect, when added to the real cash outflow produced by the venture in its early life, is in practice a step too far for many firms. It often drives companies to use an IPO to get an external valuation to set against losses, to seek a joint venture partner, or to find some other way of getting the venture off its P & L.

Phantom options

These are a form of bonus that work like options but lead to the delivery of cash rather than equity, and were used in the dotcom boom because they provide alignment without forcing the parent to relinquish total control and endure the accounting 'hit' just described. The downside is that they are complex. They require a periodic valuation of the venture which can be achieved only by a formula or by an external valuation. Furthermore, the valuation method has to be stipulated in advance to avoid any temptation on the parent or venture management to bend the consultant process their way. All of this may be too complicated in relation to the benefits it brings.

In our experience, bonuses work best, and they are preferred in most of the firms we have spoken to. A good venture management can tie the award of bonuses to specific targets selected for their positive correlation with business value. In the short term, these targets are usually in product development and sales; in the medium term, they are revenues; and in the longer term they are earnings. In this way, the poor alignment performance of bonuses can be mitigated.

Relationship to parent

New businesses need attention. Business plans change, new management comes in and deadlines come thick and fast. A line manager, as we saw in the Decadia example above, cannot deal with this alone. A good non-executive board is composed of executives on the venture review board, as we saw at Roche Diagnostics. Powergen moves senior managers on the venture review board gradually into a venture non-executive role and adds external venture capitalists to the mix.

The business plan on which the venture was funded is the contract between the business and its owners, regardless of who those owners are. A good corporate business plan contains targets and deadlines by which venture management can be given incentives and its performance managed. The venture's non-executive board steers the subsidiary through these stages and continually reviews whether the business is viable and whether it should be integrated into the firm, sold, floated or injected into a joint venture.

As the venture develops, business models and strategies change and targets need modification. Again, the board looks after this on behalf of the company, just as the company itself looks after its divisions and non-integrated subsidiaries. At the same time, the board continually reviews the performance, and the positions, of the venture management team.

CONCLUSION

In this chapter we have made six major points about the Set-up stage:

- Apart from closure and sale, the parent company has four ownership choices for a new venture, spread across a spectrum of percentage ownership. Two of these are spin-in, and the other two are spin-out.

- The funding and positioning of the venture depends on its financial attractiveness, strategic fit and strategic importance. The first two of these take us full circle back to the business development model. Usually all three criteria have to be passed for a venture to receive funding.

- P & L-focused business units and divisions do not make a good home for loss-making ventures. Instead, for spin-in candidates, a subsidiary may be a more suitable option.

- The main issues when setting up a subsidiary are the transfer of staff, remuneration and incentives, and the relationship to the parent company.

- For spin-ins, bonuses work better than the other incentive options. Their poor alignment performance can be mitigated through careful selection of targets.

- For spin-ins, a non-executive board manages the new venture on behalf of the parent company.

12 The Corporate Entrepreneur

In the 1480s Christopher Columbus believed that with some money and a good wind he could reach India going west from Europe. With the promise of untold riches when he returned he asked the King of Portugal to fund him. The king was no fool, however, and knew that he was getting a better return on investment from trips down the African coast. Columbus decided to try his hand with the House of Spain and approached Queen Isabella of Castile, but she and her husband Ferdinand, the King of Aragon, also refused to help. Christopher, a former resident of Lisbon, knew that Isabella came from Portuguese royalty and worked his way into her affections by sprinkling his Spanish with a few Portuguese phrases. When she found out in 1486 that he was looking to finance his voyage privately, Isabella began paying him stipends not to take his plan elsewhere. Finally, at the third try, Christopher convinced her to give him two million maravedis and 90 sailors and to persuade the city of Palos to give him three ships – *Nina*, *Pinta* and *Santa Maria*. The trip was almost a disaster, but Columbus eventually returned with parrots, pearls and of course gold. The monarchs became rich, but their enthusiasm for Christopher ebbed as the years passed. By 1500 he had been imprisoned and shipped back to Spain.

Half a millennium later, little has changed. The entrepreneur offers up his idea, struggles to get funding, and eventually makes the venture happen through guile, drive and hard work and at great personal risk. Then someone in management grabs it and the entrepreneur is forgotten.

These corporate entrepreneurs are the driving force behind business creation and they need to be found and encouraged. Each company has to understand who they are, what motivates them and how they think. How does a company find its corporate Columbuses and what do they need to be successful? By looking at how good corporate entrepreneurs formulate their approach and build their ventures we can help would-be entrepreneurs in *Ad Hoc* firms and provide managers in *Focused* companies with the insights they need to organize their business creation processes.

GETTING NOTICED

Suggestion boxes are usually the death of good ideas. Mixed in with complaints, abuse and naïve tirades about the colour of the office walls, a good idea has no hope of being seen. If a company's approach to sourcing ideas is so limited, any self-respecting entrepreneur will avoid this method anyway. Similarly, the executive responsible for reading suggestions knows what really happens. 'If it comes in the suggestion box,' thinks the executive, 'then it must be worthless.'

How, then, does an entrepreneur gain the attention of a company? Consider the case of Keith Hollender, an entrepreneur who developed the concept of an Unclaimed Asset Register, which he then sold to insurance broker Aon (see Example 12.1). Although Hollender was an outsider moving in, an entrepreneur inside a company with a business idea would do well to follow his example. He did the opposite of using the suggestion box. Instead, he established what he was trying to do, worked out what he needed in order to do it, and then he negotiated himself a position with the company best placed to help him.

Example 12.1 Keith Hollender and Aon (1)

In 1990, prompted by a friend's suggestion that many listed firms sit on dividends that they are unable to distribute due to incorrect share registers, Keith Hollender approached UK share registrars to discuss the possibility of setting up a public database of lost dividends. Built around account holders' names and last known addresses, the product would allow individuals to see whether any of the institutions held assets in their name and then bring the two parties together. The registrars were otherwise occupied however and had no time for him or his idea.

Five years later, Hollender tried again. This time, he realized that this was a business which could not be started by a group of individuals. To work, it had to have the co-operation of big firms which would be loath to part with information from their customer databases unless they were dealing with another large company which they could successfully sue if things went wrong. The friend put Hollender in touch with insurance firm Aon, which had already set up a similar business – the Art Loss Register – to help insurers to track down stolen art and thereby save on claims. Aon quickly understood Hollender's proposal and, in May 1998, recruited him to carry out a feasibility study.

Hollender worked-up his proposition, Unclaimed Assets Register (UAR), as far as he could. He researched the background to the opportunity, including the breakdown by asset type and the existing schemes to match owners with assets. He established the legal barriers that UAR would have to surmount, and consulted a wide variety of consumer and trade associations, government departments and regulators. Finally, Hollender proved that both data contributors and searchers would be prepared to pay fees and that UAR could simply introduce them to each other. By this time the types of 'lost assets' had expanded to cover life policies, pensions, dormant accounts and National Savings, whose collective scale was estimated at £6 billion.

Taking the idea forward required capital and the overt backing of a blue-chip company. At a time of falling insurance rates, Aon was willing to invest in new ventures. Hollender agreed to go on the payroll and become a corporate entrepreneur.

More generally, just because an entrepreneur is working in a particular company does not make that company the most suitable vehicle with which to develop the idea. In fact, using that company may retard it. Beyond that, an outsider submitting an idea does so as a partner, not as an employee, and a company considering it does so as an investor, not as an employer. So the would-be entrepreneur, whether inside a firm or outside it, should think like an outsider – like Keith Hollender, in fact. We recommend a five-step process:

- Work-up the idea and produce a proposal.

- Test the idea with mentors and friends.

- Analyse motivation and establish personal goals.

- Research and rank target companies.

- Choose a company and formulate an approach.

Working up the idea

The tough entrepreneur works up his idea to the best of his ability and resources before contacting anyone about it. He does this by turning his idea into a proposal, so that he gives his target the information he or she needs to give him an answer. Otherwise the target will just say 'no', which is always easier than reviewing the idea.

When the company looks at the idea it is looking at the person too, so the entrepreneur is selling himself as well as the concept. A well-researched, well-written proposal improves the terms of trade and makes the owner look professional and expert. If the entrepreneur has already added value to the idea by making it into a proposal, then the chances are that he can carry on adding value.

In Chapter 9 we detailed how to work an idea up to the point where it becomes a proposal for Seed investment. Much of this work involves spending no money, and the entrepreneur can often do it by himself or with the help of some friends or colleagues. The proposal has to be data-grounded, the customer proposition and product concept clear and convincing and the financials attractive. All of this can be written up in 3000 words.

Finally, the entrepreneur needs to work out what business assets would give him an unfair advantage over the competition. What three things that he does not have would he most like? Perhaps an army of sales people will get him started, or maybe a large product development team experienced in this kind of product. This analysis is central to his choice of partner. If there is nothing he needs, then there is no value in a partner and he can get going by himself. If he only needs money, then angel investors or remortgaging his home may well be better choices than working with a company.

Testing the idea

Before searching for an audience, the entrepreneur needs to find some mentors to review and comment on his proposal. This should be a varied audience to capture different perspectives, with at least a couple of experienced businesspeople who understand the nature of business plans. Those selected must be trustworthy and be able to have both a strategic and a practical view of the proposal. The assembled group must be able to offer the entrepreneur the friendly but devastating criticism of his proposal that he needs to improve it. Only after several iterations of such criticism will the proposal be ready for dispatch to a decision-making executive.

Self analysis

There are three ways of working-up a venture with a company: as an employee, in a spin-out, or with the company as an investor in the business. The driver is the entrepreneur's risk/reward profile. The more control and money he desires, the more he ought to be disinclined to work with a company as an employee.

He should therefore consider his own motivations and goals in developing the opportunity. These are central to the negotiations with the company, and enable the entrepreneur to formulate an approach that does not reveal to his counterpart what motivates him. Take the example of Daniel Guermeur, an IT manager at Schlumberger who developed an idea for a new software product. While he flirted with the idea of setting out on his own, he ultimately chose to stay with Schlumberger rather than move 'out with the hyenas' (see Example 12.2).

Example 12.2 Daniel Guermeur and Schlumberger

Daniel Guermeur had worked at Schlumberger in France for 15 years. As IT manager within a $3 billion revenues product group, he had become familiar with the software installation engineering centre in Austin, Texas. The frustrations he encountered while trying to deal with that group started him thinking about an idea to improve the situation. This idea was for a software kit to enable non-technical people to create an online communications environment using messaging, whiteboards, email and presentation tools tailored to their specific type of work. Each user could then publish the software to collaborators.

At the outset Guermeur wanted to go it alone. So he developed most of the software himself over 9 months outside company time and then posted it on the Internet as open source. After the 10 000th download he realized that he was on to something and that he should take it more seriously. He obtained a transfer to Austin and started weighing-up his options. Venture capital was plentiful but venture capitalists were aggressive, and Schlumberger looked bureaucratic and was not focused on his target clients.

Guermeur thought long and hard about leaving the protective shell of the company and seeking his fortune with the venture capitalists, but in the end he decided to stay with Schlumberger as a primary investor because he preferred a 'big uncle' to look after him rather than to be 'out with the hyenas'. He realized that Schlumberger had, 'a brand that would do wonders for me, open doors, get me lower prices and possibly get me customers'.

Like David Guermeur, the entrepreneur needs to be clear about his own motivation and be sure that the projects fits with his personal risk–reward profile. He needs to be confident that he is truly an entrepreneur, and not just someone who wants a new and more exciting job. He also has to be clear why he has not left the company to pursue the idea. If he is an outsider, it is important that he identifies what it is he really wants – a job, a partner, or an investor. His motivation will be different from that of the insider. It may be the possibility of real wealth, or any of fun, independence, experience and learning, fame, power and expressing his creativity.

He has to be honest. He must ask people who know him. What are his wants and needs? He must look at his own history of risk taking and the key decisions he has taken in his life. Only when he understands his desire for risk and reward, control and money can he choose a whether to work with a company or not.

Researching companies

In order to be on the entrepreneur's list of possibilities, a company should have one or more of the business assets he needs to succeed. Web search and specialist database products between them enable him to compile a list of suitable firms. He can search for each firm's strategy statements from the CEO and in its financial reports, compile investment selection criteria and score his idea against them to see whether it matches.

The entrepreneur has to work out what assets the company has in terms of market channels, operational and product capabilities, processes, factories, production centres, brand, know-how, or just experience. Then he has to find the answer to the question: does the company have what he needs? By ranking each company on assets, he should be able to pick one firm. Who knows, it may even be the one he already works for.

Next, he has to work out how the company manages its ventures. He needs to understand its position on the business creation model and its business creation mode (Chapters 3 and 4) and then decide whether it and the corporate culture can cope with his kind of venture. He will have to find people at the company willing to talk. If he is in the company already, he can have a confidential talk with someone with a strategic view.

Approach

Once the entrepreneur has matched his idea to a company, has looked at himself and researched the company's venturing style, he is in a good position to make an approach and open negotiations. More research will have to be done to ascertain the right people to approach and whether now is the best time to approach them. Keith Hollender, the entrepreneur we introduced earlier, has a word of warning here.

> I would advise a corporate entrepreneur to think first whether you need a company at all. UAR had to have help, but many business ideas don't. The hardest part is matching an entrepreneurial idea with an established company. Companies are not stuffed full with entrepreneurial people who are willing to risk their careers. I was fortunate with Aon.
>
> If you are doing a venture outside, the concern is money. Dealing with banks and lenders and overdrafts is awful. Inside a company the politics are bad but the money is basically there. So, you swap money for politics. Take your pick.

ENTREPRENEURS INSIDE *AD HOC* FIRMS

The biggest problems for entrepreneurs occur in *Ad Hoc* firms. In *Focused* firms, venture units (or their equivalent) operate a system and in *Integrated* firms the system is absorbed into the companies' everyday practices. *Ad Hoc* firms have neither a business creation system nor a supportive culture, so that managers and the entrepreneur come into direct, unmediated contact and often end up fighting it out. 'All that is stopping me,' says Erik Findeisen, a corporate entrepreneur at Quebecor, 'is a mixture of capital, the economy and culture'.

We tackle this environment in the second half of this chapter. Many brave souls have tried to work 'inside the beast', and many more have no choice but to do so. We present the lessons that their forerunners have learned, some of which are also useful for those working inside *Focused* and even *Integrated* firms. The experiences of entrepreneurs in this type of company provide seven lessons. How do they do it?

■   Find a sponsor to provide management cover and money.

■   Keep costs low by begging, borrowing and stealing equipment and help.

■   'Just do it' by asking for permission only when necessary.

■   Lobby to make the venture harder to kill than to support or tolerate.

■   Pick the battles by playing the game and fighting only to save the project.

■   Balance risk–reward by taking only sensible risks.

■   Maintain alternatives in case the project suddenly ends.

Finding a sponsor

Entrepreneurs need a senior management sponsor, ideally from strategy or business development, to provide both money and cover for the venture in the way that the venture unit does in *Focused* firms. Without money the venture cannot proceed beyond the paper stage, and without cover it is constantly vulnerable to changes in management perspective and priority.

Michel Lefevre, the manager of the Accountancy Portal project described in Chapter 5, never found a sponsor. Instead, he and his team only enjoyed the acquiescence of their managers. 'Nobody said it was a bad idea or that it didn't fit with the company strategy. We were never given a formal no. Nor were we given a formal yes.' The result was slow access to capital and interminable micromanagement.

Keeping costs low

In major companies, big is often beautiful. Financial and human resources are regularly used and abused on a vast scale. Projects can take on large staffs and spend monstrous budgets, in keeping with Stuart Degg's (Royal & SunAlliance) observation that management is generally measured on 'acreage and heads of cattle'. In venturing, however, small is beautiful, particularly when it comes to money (Example 12.3). One venture executive says, 'We performed magic. We made $40 000 last three times as long as expected. The company couldn't believe it. We travelled cheaply and only when really necessary and we had no excess anywhere.'

Example 12.3   Keith Hollender and Aon (2)

Knowing nothing of Aon's culture and processes, and with the sponsorship of a single executive, Keith Hollender set about building his business as cheaply as possible. Within a month he had persuaded a law firm to provide £15 000 worth of legal advice on data protection free of charge. In order to escape the attentions of finance, he did not prepare a budget. His first hire came more than a year after he had started, and development of the UAR service was carried out by an external contractor at a cost of only £200 000, a sum lower than many companies would have spent on consultants to do a technology feasibility study.

Keith says of his parsimonious style, 'I have done this on a shoestring. That means that people don't get excited and complain. Try to do things too quickly, too flashily, and people panic.' Hollender got involved in all aspects of the venture, co-designing the UAR interface, working-up the legal contracts with 15 data providers, writing all the business and financial plans, and devising and executing UAR's marketing strategy. For a period, when Aon's B2B-style finance department could not keep up with the flow of cheques for the £18 database search fee, Hollender did his own double-entry bookkeeping.

A wide variety of methods is available to the enterprising venture team. To start with, the buying power of large firms is such that many suppliers are prepared to provide free goods and services to a venture in return for an introduction to the firm's buyer or simply as a loss-leader. A canny venture team also develops the ability to milk its host company of help and material. The likelihood is that by the time anybody notices, the venture has been financed or has failed. Office space and computers are often idle and can be borrowed.

Entrepreneurial middle management staff in marketing and business development love to help out a venture team, because if the venture gets going good jobs may become available. There is no stopping such moonlighting, as many corporate middle management staff are unsupervised from week to week. Should line management refuse to allocate a vital member of staff to the venture, then this person can help out anyway in his spare time. When the project has won 'official' status, management applies an authoritative rubber stamp to what is happening anyway.

Just do it

Once a venture team has found its sponsor then it has the finance, the space and the authority to get on with it. There is no excuse for hanging around waiting for instructions (see Example 12.4).

Example 12.4   Keith Hollender and Aon (3)

In 2001, its first full year of operation, UAR generated £400 000 in revenue for Aon. By March 2002, the 5-year forecast indicated an annual revenue opportunity of £15 million with high margins. With strong lock-in effects creating a barrier to entry to competitors, UAR was a great little business set for strong growth, and in mid-2002 Aon sold it on to database firm Experian.

Looking back on the 3-year development phase at Aon, Keith Hollender says: 'I asked permission to do things as infrequently as possible and engaged in what I call presumptive taking. I rode on

Aon's back as much as I could. I was careful about it of course, getting advice in a number of instances, but it was one of the reasons I had joined in the first place. Overall, I had little interference because I kept UAR deliberately small. Large companies are not coherent or monolithic places, and there are ways to do basically whatever you want.'

Keith Hollender puts his finger here on the cold logic of corporate entrepreneurship inside the *Ad Hoc* firm: once the venture team is committed to its venture it has nothing to lose. If the venture works, then failure to adhere to procedure is generally forgiven. If the venture fails, then the team's crimes against bureaucracy are minor compared with the sins of crashing the business, wasting money and making the sponsor look bad.

Lobby hard

The determining factor in the progress of a venture in an *Ad Hoc* firm venture is the support of potential customers and the firm's top management (see Example 12.5). In such firms, inertia acts as a brake against new activities and ways of doing things. A favourite trick of the skilled entrepreneur is to turn that inertia to his advantage so that it becomes harder for the company not to do the venture than it is to do it – remember Christopher Columbus.

Example 12.5   Keith Hollender and Aon (4)

Soon after starting, Keith Hollender began a twin-track marketing campaign to brand UAR as a combination of a public service and a public lottery that produced windfalls. The first track was to use the media. By the end of summer 1998, Hollender had already appeared on BBC Radio 4 and in the personal finance sections of major UK daily newspapers, and over the next 3 years he made more than 150 media appearances, some of these featuring individuals that the UAR had helped find assets that they never knew they had.

The second track of the campaign was to win support from external organizations. The UK financial regulator (the Authority) Financial Services was one, ProShare (a share ownership and financial education organization) was another. In an inspired move, Hollender decided to donate a proportion of the venture's revenues to charity. This won the endorsements of the charities concerned and further branded UAR as a public good.

The marketing campaign cost UAR and Aon little and successfully built awareness of the service among consumers. It also built awareness of the service inside Aon. 'People keep coming up to me saying they have seen me in the paper', says Keith. 'The upshot is that UAR is generally perceived here to be a good thing that adds to the brand equity of the company.'

Keith Hollender cleverly used a combination of publicity and constituency-building to make inertia work for him. Another method is to line up a joint venture partner. The Accountancy Portal team found that having such a partner helped it overcome management doubts about the project (although the project failed in the end). 'Somebody else was interested in risking money on our idea and suddenly there were other people for management to say no to', says the venture team manager.

In the end it is a question of balance. Daniel Guermeur from Metadot says of his relationship with Schlumberger, 'You end up feeling like you are coaching the company about how to run a start-up business. The key is to minimize the influence of the parent while keeping it happy.'

Choose battles

An ancient Chinese proverb holds that the wise man travelling uphill does not climb trees. The wise corporate entrepreneur does not confront the company unnecessarily. Instead, he obediently complies with procedure – forms, reporting and budgets – wherever possible and when he disobeys he does so stealthily.

Companies generally do not make concessions to ventures on IPR and equity. Audit and inspection by business process people, when they occur, are compulsory and unavoidable. Corporate entrepreneurs we have interviewed are unanimous that none of these was worth fighting, although some of them did fight at the time.

Balance risk–reward

Although venturing is risky, the upside for venture team members can be substantial. Working in Diageo, a *Focused* firm with a venture unit, Rupert Markland has opted not to pursue the issues of IPR, equity and his own personal future. When asked about his motivation for doing the Guinness Good Times project, Markland mentions learning, freedom and fun. His main goal, he says, was to broaden his business experience and get 'closer to the coalface'. In his 18 months in GGT, Markland has effectively done a full on-the-job MBA, specializing in consumer marketing, contract negotiation and human resource management. He has also acquired skills not taught on the usual MBA: persuasion selling, budgeting and project management, business planning and resource gathering. He has the satisfaction of having created a new business and, lastly, enjoys a wider range of career opportunities than before he started on GGT.

The Accountancy Portal executive agrees: 'I learned a lot and would do it again for that. Market research was new to me and I learned about how to do venture project management and how to write a comprehensive business plan. I even waited by a lift for a senior manager to chance by. Now I'm not afraid to sell to people.'

These two examples highlight the learning bargain between company and the venture team in the development of a venture. The venture team delivers a ready-made venture in exchange for the learning gained while working on it, while the company spends money to learn about the opportunity to decide whether to execute it or not.

Maintain alternatives

Ventures can end suddenly. Money can be denied, a key colleague can decide to leave, or a fatal flaw in the proposition can suddenly turn up. One of the definitions of the *Ad Hoc* company is that it does not provide a mechanism for limiting a venture team's downside. Therefore, the team has to look after itself.

One remedy is to find alternative financing to develop the venture should the company back out. Venture capitalists do not usually deal with ventures before revenues are flowing and are often reluctant to invest in corporate propositions. The best alternative funding source is a supplier, a customer or a joint venture partner. The Accountancy Portal executive rues his late start in this area: 'I tried all the financing options. At the end I tried to turn it into a three-cornered joint venture. But I didn't have very long as I only started when it became clear that the company wasn't going to fund the venture further. So, reluctantly, I have parked the idea and will return to it when the time is right.'

The second remedy is to have another job ready to go to should the worst happen. This is good for an individual's bargaining position. Also, because it helps him relax into the venture as it develops, it helps him treat the company as a partner rather than as an employer.

CONCLUSION

In this chapter we have made three major points about corporate entrepreneurship which are of use to both entrepreneurs and managers:

■   Suggesting an idea is unlikely to be successful. The would-be corporate entrepreneur is better served by adopting a structured approach to building the idea and finding a corporate partner if necessary.

■ Before approaching a company (including an employer), the entrepreneur should assess the firm's suitability for his venture (see the business creation model in Chapters 3 and 4).

■ Working inside an *Ad Hoc* firm, an entrepreneur must steer a course that is both cautious and bold and protect both the project and himself.

Section 3

Integrated Business Creation

13 Remaining Focused

CAUTIONARY TALES

In the heart of this book we detailed how a company can organize itself for business creation. By operating a system by which ventures are selected, funded and developed, and initially vesting that system in a venture unit or similar, a firm can begin to develop the business creation capability to the point where it is *Focused* according to our definitions in Chapter 4.

Remaining *Focused* is not easy for the firm that has started out in venturing. Any of a number of things can go wrong and cause venturing to die before it has had a chance to become embedded in the culture and practices of the firm. The result is that during the years 2000–2002 internal venturing flowered briefly in several companies and then expired. Other companies, however, ploughed through changes in mood regardless. Examples 13.1 and 13.2 illustrate how the border between success and failure is narrow and marked by one or two key decisions.

Example 13.1 Cyntec's failed business creation initiative

Colin Rathbone, Strategy Director at Cyntec, started venturing at the 70 000-employee global firm in 2000 with the CEO's support and £175 million to establish a new venture unit. The remit was to achieve 100 per cent return in 3 years by reusing Cyntec's R & D assets to create new businesses, to establish a process for innovative thinking and renewal, and then to disband after embedding this process across the firm. Rathbone recruited 18 staff and set up a big new office with enough space for 15 venture teams.

In his first year, Rathbone concentrated on generating and developing internal ideas. He spent £30 million on setting-up and developing eight proposals, taking three to launch. By March 2001, over 30 staff worked in the unit. Of these, 12 did venture development, four were finance specialists, two were marketing specialists, one was an IT specialist, three were management and the remainder were support executives. According to another executive in the group, however, the team centred excessively on idea generation but found few that were suitable and, moreover, did not have the skills to develop them.

Rathbone responded to this by switching to ideas from outside the company. The unit toured venture capitalists and investment banks to look for JV and investment opportunities with the intention of bartering assistance and access to Cyntec's business assets for equity. Soon, it was overwhelmed by business plans from outside, and venture capitalists started to ask for guidance on the ideas they should submit. In July 2001, in response to requests for strategic direction, Rathbone reorganized the group into sub-groups and reduced staffing to 15.

Later in 2001, a new Chief Operating Officer started work at Cyntec. The company decided to focus on its core activities and the business creation part of the original remit was downplayed in favour of the innovative thinking element. Although the group attempted to turn itself into an internal consultancy, venturing ended in November 2001. During the period of the unit's existence, 500 ideas had been received, 50 started, 20 seeded and seven invested, and £65 million had been spent overall.

Looking back on the experience in mid-2002, Rathbone says, 'The concentration on external ideas took us away from internal ones and that was a mistake. Our skills lay in recombining the core business and we never made a success with ideas from outside. We made some money and we created a capability, but we did not embed it – ventures DNA is not now intertwined with that of Cyntec.'

What went wrong at Cyntec? The initial brief was textbook perfect. The mission was to 'create, embed and disband', the focus was on the core business, and CEO commitment in the shape of £175 million was unequivocal. Compare this story from a similarly sized company, British American Tobacco (BAT).

Example 13.2   Business creation at BAT

Internal venturing started in the tobacco firm BAT in January 2000 with a number of creative thinking sessions about how new information technologies would alter the pattern of operations and create new business opportunities. This resulted in BAT's top management giving an IT executive, Phil Colman, and an operating unit manager, Jeremy Pike, the task of leading the exploitation of e-business opportunities. With a presence in most countries, around 80 manufacturing units and several major international brands, BAT was a global, vertically integrated company with plenty of scope for business innovation.

With a first-year set-up budget of £12 million, Colman and Pike recruited a dozen up-and-coming managers from the firm's 80 000 staff and set up a venture unit named Imagine & Evolution (I&E) a tactful distance from the corporate centre in London. One sub-group, Imagine, was to generate and select ideas, and the other, Evolution, was to develop and implement them. Having created an open, interactive working environment different from corporate headquarters, the group was well set to focus on areas in and around the core business and to create a new stream of businesses.

Within a year, the group had found that getting results was harder than anyone had expected. Rolling smart ideas out into BAT's end-markets was impossible without the help and acceptance of the functional teams, but securing this took time. The 10 people originally in Evolution were not enough to deal with the end-markets that BAT served and the unit could not spin things out without the help of another group – Business Development – which reported to the CEO and was biased towards the acquisition of other tobacco players. Last but not least, according to Colman, 'Dot-bomb meant that the company's appetite for spin-outs was very small.'

Operating a standalone group specializing in 'new stuff' was not working well enough, so BAT executives decided to redirect I&E closer to its core business. In July 2001, they appointed a Business Development Director and placed both I&E and Business Development (renamed Acquisitions & Ventures) under him, adding Strategy later on in 2001. I&E then changed its modus operandi. Instead of producing, as Colman puts it, 'bright shiny new things', it became 'like liquid', finding areas where it could act as an internal venture consultant and partner to opportunities within BAT. I&E was assisted by its alumni across the company, who acted as evangelists for venturing and provided links across the company structure. Under this arrangement, BAT's central groups became internal customers and had to buy into an opportunity before a major funding request went to the board. This kept the group focused and ensured that weaker ideas did not survive.

This process was pursued during 2001 when Colman and Pike restructured I&E to align closely with BAT's functional structure. Looking back, Colman is proud of what they did. 'We shook BAT into life on e-business, created an environment where ideas were welcomed and encouraged, managed to hold on to some frustrated but creative people, and produced two major ventures and several internal initiatives', he says.

During 2002 I&E recognized that its efforts needed to be placed in the context of an overall enterprise plan. As an indication of how the venture unit had transformed itself from its e-business days into an organic strategy-led venture capability, I&E relocated to corporate headquarters and retitled itself 'Enterprise Development'. Its close links with group strategy now allow it to, in Colman's words, 'fit venturing solidly into BAT's strategic processes so that we develop ideas that fit the enterprise plan.'

LESSONS

The similarities between BAT and Cyntec are striking. They started venturing on almost the same day, both with senior management commitment and separate venture units that contained the firms' elite staff. Each produced a respectable number of ventures and changed tack after 12–15 months. However, one thrived, and the other did not. We now proceed to identify the differences and draw some conclusions from them.

Moderate speed and cost

Diageo's Raphael Offer has a motto: 'One can get a lot done for less.' We have found that cost is the main determinant of the survival of venturing in *Focused* firms. This is because the time horizons of venturing are long and because the cost goes straight to the bottom line. It is a while until the first venture makes an operating profit, and a long while until the total operating profit of all new ventures exceeds the current costs of creating new ones so that venturing itself becomes cash flow positive. Finally, yet later still, the profits made by operating ventures exceed the total costs of creating them, running the venture unit, and creating and closing the ventures that did not make it. Only at this point has venturing broken even.

For a long time, therefore, business creation is a cost centre. All business people know that cost centres have to keep their heads down. So, small is beautiful in the land of venturing. When the Chief Operating Officer gets his cost-cutting cudgel out, which *Focused* venture unit is going to survive – the one that quietly spends $3 million producing two ventures a year, or the one that spends $20 million a year producing four?

Let us go back to Cyntec. In 2 years, its venture unit spent £65 million and went from a headcount of 15 to over 30, then back to zero. Given a prior public CEO commitment of £175 million, this unit was going to spend money at a ferocious rate. A new office with new computers and no fewer than eight service personnel – more than exist in most other venture units we have looked at – are testimony to the lack of cost control in this operation. BAT's unit, by contrast, was authorized to go to 25 staff but never did so. It spent £12 million in its first, set-up year and £8.5 million in the next – or around one-third of the amount spent by Cyntec for roughly the same level of venturing activity.

Let us look at it another way. Fixed operating costs pay for the established staff in the unit to operate the venturing system and to help get quality ventures up and running within it. Venture costs pay for actual venture development before investment. This suggests a small venture unit team. One business creation executive says, 'Keep the operation low fixed-cost, big variable-cost. This way you avoid blowing the internal finance system. I didn't need a marketing person in each team, for instance. I preferred to hire them at the time of investment. In general I kept core in-house people to a minimum and used outside consultants. Not people like McKinsey, but specialists. It's a great way of recruiting people.' Diageo, Roche Diagnostics and Powergen, too, operate according to this pattern.

From a bottom–up perspective, we have previously shown that the cost of producing a venture should fall between 1 and 3 per cent of the expected annual revenues of the new business. Costs often fall to the lower end of this range, especially for larger ventures and for those where product development is deferred until after investment. Using a figure of 2 per cent suggests that the total revenue opportunity provided to the firm per year by a venture unit costing 0.1 per cent of company revenues is around 5 per cent of those revenues, with positive scaling effects. Powergen, Diageo and Lloyds TSB all venture steadily on budgets at around this proportion of their revenues. This analysis shows that careful, strategic selection of ventures on a case-by-case basis and low-cost development to the point of investment decision together allow a firm to match its activities to its opportunities, and that large dedicated funds and short-term investment targets do not.

Where does speed come in? Excessive speed is generally bad in venturing, especially at the beginning when the capability is protean and unable to withstand harsh tests. Few venture units have much idea what they are doing in their first year – Cyntec and BAT both changed tack at the 1-year point – and the less money spent during that period the less will be wasted and the smaller the adverse reaction from other corporate divisions. Powergen's Spark unit provides a useful model. Run cautiously by Tim Forrest for 18 months, the unit used specialist consultants at the outset to define its process and has started modestly with one very small and one medium-sized venture. Forrest says, 'We are a lean, low-budget operation, not spending wildly. We can scale-up should a big opportunity come winging by, but we won't until it does.'

Stay close to core

Once the first year was over at BAT and Cyntec, each manager took stock of the situation. The dotcom boom was over. Finding, selecting and developing opportunities was not as easy as had been expected, and tens of millions had been spent. They both had to make a choice. BAT consolidated, moving back towards its core and building relationships with central and geographic groups in order to gain access to BAT's marketing and operational assets. Cyntec, in contrast, diversified. It started to look outside the firm for more and better opportunities, and rapidly tried to build an external investment activity without the benefit of strong links to its existing assets, forcing another reorganization. The unit failed to build a company-wide constituency, with the result that few mourned when the COO wielded the axe.

Venture units that stray away from the company's core tend not to survive because they deliver few strategic benefits. An interesting example is BG Group's corporate development programme (see Example 13.3). Directed by Stephen Brandon, a senior executive, it invested in a series of promising internal ventures.

Example 13.3   Corporate development at BG Group

In February 1999 senior management at BG Group carried out a strategy review and found that the portfolio of investment projects within the core businesses (International Exploration & Production – now BG – and UK Transmission and Distribution – now Lattice) would not enable the company to achieve its goal of top quartile performance, which implied a 15 per cent annual increase in earnings over the next 5 years. The time horizons of the investments, they discovered, were on average too long. Executives wrestled with this 'growth gap', and decided to form a Corporate Development Group (CDG) under director Stephen Brandon to attempt to deliver net income of £500 million within 5 years from new, non-core business. According to Brandon, 'The target was crude, but indicated the importance of the effort. It was intended that I should leverage the company's assets, skills and cash flow. It was also clear that we were to develop rather than buy, although M & A opportunities could be considered.'

CDG ran through a standard process of idea generation and selection and produced 10 initial projects, including the mobile telecoms masts venture that we featured in Chapter 10. Other projects included natural gas vehicles, home refuelling with compressed natural gas, and a new type of boiler to generate electricity from gas in the home. Brandon hired into the group a number of executives from within BG Group and outside it, some to work with ventures and others to work on venture unit activities.

By the end of 1999 Brandon realized that mobile telecoms masts was the only one of the 10 projects likely to deliver an early and material contribution to value. In the meantime, BG Group decided to split itself into BG and Lattice, each of which subsequently gained its own stock market quotation. As a central function, the position of the venture unit was precarious and, inevitably, it was broken up. Neither of the two CEOs wished to retain the capability that Brandon had built up, in spite of their commitments to growth in their new companies.

Each of the ventures went to one or other of the successor companies or was closed. The same happened to each of CDG's staff.

The two telecoms projects and most of the CDG team were taken by Lattice, which invested further in both until the telecoms collapse. According to another former BG Group executive, life in the demerged BG became tougher and tougher. First, the development of new ventures was stopped. Second, BG's rigorous financial processes were not suitable for ventures in their growth phase and stymied their development. All in all, although BG carried on developing a couple of ventures in operating units overseas, it was unable to manage operational and investment business separately.

Although this is an unusual story of a venture unit stranded by changes in its host company, we can see that the Corporate Development Group's focus on non-core ventures contributed to the demise of the capability, certainly within the BG division. This harks back to our point about firms needing to venture for both strategic and financial benefits if the capability is not ultimately to be lost. When offered the opportunity to take on the Corporate Development Group's business creation capability, both the Lattice and BG CEOs declined to do so. Such a unit ran contrary to their goals of maintaining a track record of profits, and its strategic benefits were judged not to be justifiable. In general, financial benefits tend to be one-off – thanks, and goodbye.

Another fine example of this tendency is British Airways. Notwithstanding 11 years of successful venturing that took in seven new businesses including executive jet chartering, two B2B carve-outs in in-flight retailing and back-office operations, an airline consultancy, and finally the London Eye, British Airways was hit by a downturn in 2001. Rod Eddington arrived with a mission to restore the profitability of the airline operation, and venturing was a casualty.

The lesson from all these experiences is summed up by Raphael Offer again: 'Stay close to the core business. This is one of the secrets of continued success.' Organizational separation of ventures and backing from senior management through a venture review board solves the problem of cultural resistance from operating units but does not mean that the venture unit has to focus on non-core ventures. By including ventures that are right at the heart of the company, and using those to deliver value to divisions and to nurture relationships with their executives, the venture unit improves its chances of survival in adverse circumstances.

In Chapter 7 we identified pipeline management as one of the most important tasks of the venture unit once it has established its modus operandi. A judicious mixture of ventures small and large, core and non-core, which are spread across the firm's assets, using some and extending others, satisfies the various constituencies within the firm and allows the venture unit to track movements in strategy and political imperatives and shifts in mood between investment and operations.

Get connected

We have alluded to connections and relationships throughout the book. We have shown how the venture unit can please manager and entrepreneur by using a venturing system and by being neutral and transparent. We described how to connect the venturing activity to senior management through both membership of the venture review board and reporting relationships and we advised the corporate entrepreneur that lobbying is half the story. The situations at Cyntec and BAT are stark: Colin Rathbone now regrets becoming separated from the corporate centre in the latter stages of his venturing experience, while Phil Colman depends on his unit's relationships for generating new opportunities to provide value to BAT's businesses, and plans to get back to Head Office.

Top management involvement is essential to embed venturing in the firm as it goes through the *Focused* stage. At Roche Diagnostics, Powergen, Becton Dickinson, Lloyds TSB and Diageo the CEO is at least a sponsor and is often actively involved. According to Michael Pearson at Lloyds TSB, 'The whole thing is driven by the CEO and Deputy CEO. Their attitude is that this is something we have to do.' This structure is repeated at many other companies, including BD and Powergen.

How can the venture unit win the support of senior management if it does not already have it? By cementing itself in the firm through marketing to its divisions. The venture units at Lloyds TSB and BAT, for instance, experienced the joy and frustration of a division taking a venture from it. Both managers learned from the experience that this is a sign of success, not failure, and an inevitable part of the process by which venturing spreads across their firms.

Notwithstanding the support and involvement of top management, Michael Pearson at Lloyds TSB spends considerable effort getting buy-in from key divisional executives, using them as a means of generating ideas and marketing Strategic Ventures across the company. Raphael Offer at Diageo considers his relationship with the divisions to be the most important aspect of his work, and is careful not to cross them. When asked what would happen if somebody came to him with a suggestion for a new Guinness drink, Offer replied that New Business Ventures (NBV) doesn't do drinks, Guinness does – 'It is clear where ideas go, and there is no conflict.' At the same time, he is concerned to share knowledge benefits generated by NBV with Diageo units across the world. One decidedly non-core venture, Nightfly – a service that delivers information about nightspots via SMS messaging – showed the Smirnoff group in Ireland how to market via SMS and taught the Great Britain division how to use CRM technology. Divisions sometimes want to emulate a central venture unit and establish one of their own. At Powergen in May 2002, after 18 months, Tim Forrest received his first phone call from a divisional colleague asking for help.

The last aspect of connection for the venture unit is its relationship with related corporate groups – M & A, alliances, and business development. Many firms lean towards off-income statement forms of business development (M & A, corporate venture capital), and the only way for a venture unit to takes its rightful place alongside acquisition and venture capital is to be organized alongside them. Otherwise, as we have illustrated, opportunities tend to arrive at senior management's door in deal form rather than being considered and then allocated to the most suitable method of business development. In Philips, the leading Dutch electronics company, for example, the head of venturing sits alongside his counterparts in alliance and M & A to ensure that they act in a complementary rather than competitive fashion.

BAT (Example 13.2), is one of the few firms where business creation did not start off as part of strategy and business development. It started, in fact, from the efforts of the IT group to define the competitive advantage that effective exploitation of IT could bring. When I&E was created its managers requested that they report direct to the owners of strategy, the Chairman and Managing Director. This was not achieved. A year later, in July 2001, they got some of what they wanted with the creation of the Business Development department covering both acquisitions and business creation. By the end of 2001, this department had taken over the strategy function.

The lesson for *Focused* companies is that those responsible for business creation must walk a fine line organizationally between the company's centre and its divisions. The more it is a tool of senior management, the more the unit has to strive to build working relationships that cement it into the organization. The closer it is to the company's divisions, the harder it must work to become or stay established at the company's centre.

Make the system flexible

The system we outlined in Section 2 works for any firm looking to develop either non-core or core business opportunities, and provides a way to generate and attract opportunities to the firm, develop them in stages to the point of investment, and position them for best effect inside or outside the firm. The system provides a means to kill ventures once a fatal flaw appears, improves the quality of development work, places each venture at arms-length from the company and thereby improves the quality of selection, and answers all the questions about HR and IPR that firms come across. It helps the venture unit reduce costs, stay close to the core, and get connected within the firm, while answering the needs of both management and entrepreneur.

To work, the system has to be neutral, transparent, helpful and trustworthy. However, at the same time, it needs to be flexible. It should be capable of accommodating many different types of ventures, and it should be managed with a light touch. Flexibility has seven main features:

- Expand and contract the venture unit and its budget to match the level of suitable opportunities.

- Allow for maverick behaviour.

- Maintain an IPR policy but be prepared to vary it.

- Maintain a standard contract for employees but be prepared to vary it.

- Accept ideas from anybody, inside and outside the firm, junior or senior.

- Look for joint venture investment funding to cover a refusal by the company to invest.

- Vary the business model – sponsor own ventures, partner with divisions on some, consult to others.

The most important of these is the first one, concerning scale. In Chapter 4 we identified the ability to move between *Emphasize* and *Ease* as a key property of *Integrated* firms. In the *Focused* mode, scale flexibility is the key to keeping costs down as it allows the unit to stay small and flex with the scale of suitable opportunities. A small unit is cheap and does not by its nature force the development of ventures in the way that a large unit does. Mature *Focused* firms therefore develop the ability to expand and contract their venturing activities.

Successful venture units also learn as they go. BAT had a difficult first year as the dotcom boom collapsed, learned a great deal and then worked out a way ahead. Powergen and Lloyds TSB are learning where to put businesses once they have emerged from their development phases.

Roche Diagnostics is perhaps the best example. After 15 months venturing, its venture unit is developing selection criteria, better HR processes and a set of decision rules to help it place ventures after development. It started out with three goals for venturing – financial and strategic benefits, learning and cultural change – and subsequently found that great care is needed when mixing them. Supporting projects for cultural and learning reasons is inconsistent with financial and strategic benefits. As a result, ventures are now selected for the latter purposes only, and cultural and learning benefits come anyway from successful venturing.

CONCLUSION

In this chapter we have made four major points about how to manage business creation:

- Moderate speed and cost. Make no upfront financial commitment. Take it easy.

- Stay close to core. Select opportunities on strategic fit and importance. Maintain a diverse portfolio of ventures.

- Get connected. Maintain relationships with management, divisions and strategy/business development.

- Operate the system flexibly. Satisfy its customers' needs. Learn as you go and be flexible. Don't overemphasize idea generation.

14 Developing an Integrated Approach

HOW FAR CAN WE TAKE THE *FOCUSED* MODE?

The *Focused* approach to business creation can be highly effective. There is an appealing logic to using a dedicated venture unit unencumbered by the bureaucracy and short-term demands of the line organization. From the executive point of view, the venture unit is the agent that takes forward business creation while management gets on and runs the business. These attitudes are not wrong. A firm *Focused* on business creation is most of the way there in terms of business creation capability. The managerial and organizational elements are in place to select and develop ventures, correct any bias towards M & A and fulfil the strategic intentions of the firm, so that ventures can be developed cheaply and untroubled by external risk.

However, the *Focused* mode also has a number of shortcomings. First, it is fragile – susceptible to changes beyond the control of the venture unit manager or even the CEO – and the business creation capability that has been so carefully nurtured can get killed-off quickly when a crisis hits. Lucent's New Venture Group is the most vivid example. It was a highly successful and widely copied operation, but when viewed in the wider context of the company's fight for survival it was only of marginal strategic value, so it had to be sold.

Second, the *Focused* mode is by definition narrow. Its primary strength as a targeted and focused activity is also its biggest weakness, because it can never reach into all the corners of the company. The result is that business creation in other parts of the firm is often stifled. As we saw in Kudu Ventures, this approach can even breed resentment in the line organization if people feel that the venture unit has the exclusive charter for all things new.

Third, the *Focused* mode typically involves some level of separation from the line organization. Again, this is both a strength and a weakness. It is a strength because separation allows venture managers to do their job without being second-guessed by corporate executives. It is a weakness because many of the strategic benefits that business creation promises rely on effective linkages to core business activities. We have seen countless cases of orphan businesses in large companies, which originally promised much but which lacked either a sponsor or an obvious fit to the existing line organization. Such cases, which often end up getting sold or killed, are testament to the problem of separation.

We have described the capability of business creation as consisting of three elements – resources, system and culture – and said that *Focused* firms are strong on resources and system but less so on cultural factors. We have also described a system of business creation and how to organize and use it. But how does this system come to be part of the firm's culture so that the two become indistinguishable?

Consider the well-worn example of quality management, and its transition from a specialized function (a 'quality department') to a distributed capability that is built in to the production process. Business creation can be viewed in the same way. It is either viewed as a separate activity off to one side, almost as an afterthought, or it is viewed as an integral part of the production function of the company. The *Integrated* mode assumes the latter – that business creation is everyone's job.

Before describing the elements of the *Integrated* mode, it is important to acknowledge its inherent risks. The most common problem with moving from the *Focused* to the *Integrated* mode is that the capability can end up being dispersed and momentum lost. An interesting example of this is GM's NUMMI (New United Motor Manufacturing Inc.) experiment. This was a joint venture factory with Toyota located in Fremont, California. Within 5 years of its establishment, NUMMI was delivering the highest levels of productivity and quality of any automobile factory in the US. But when GM came to transfer the learning from NUMMI back to its own factories, it failed. There were many factors at work, but a key problem was that the managers responsible for transferring their learning were spread too thin, and could not overcome the inertia and the 'not invented here' suspicions of the people running GM's traditional factories.

The same thing can happen in business creation. The company may have the best intentions when it decides to disband its venture unit and integrate the people and their skills into the line organization. But the key people can leave and the skills lost, thereby forcing the company back to the *Ad Hoc* mode. To varying degrees, this is what happened in Lucent, Royal & Sun Alliance and Marks & Spencer.

The other (less likely) risk with moving towards the *Integrated* mode is that business creation is taken too far, and spreads cancer-like in an uncontrollable way. Enron is the classic example a company that took the theory of creative destruction to its extreme and ultimately destroyed itself.

What does the *Integrated* mode look like? First, we should emphasize that it does *not* always mean the absence of a venture unit. Typically, there will be one or several venture units (each with a particular role) as well as a broader capability in the area of business creation. Again the analogy to quality management is instructive. Manufacturing companies typically make it clear that 'quality is everyone's job', but in addition there is still a group which is responsible for tapping into the latest ideas on quality and promulgating those ideas throughout the organization.

So, in addition to the existence of one or more venture units, the *Integrated* mode will display a dispersed business creation capability, a culture of enthusiasm and support for business creation, continued confidence and investment in business creation during lean times and of course a consistent record of creating new businesses.

THE *INTEGRATED* MODE IN PRACTICE

Let us take a detailed look at some companies that fit our concept of the *Integrated* mode. We should acknowledge here that while there are plenty of examples of companies that have moved towards it, there are few exemplars. Even companies that currently do it well are not immune to failure. As with trust and reputation, it takes a long time to build up a *Focused* business creation capability, but it can be destroyed in no time.

We describe three companies below. The first is the oil major Shell, a company operating in a mature industry characterized by continuing exploration and development of new oil and gas fields and a possible long-term shift to new forms of energy. The second is Becton Dickinson, a US-based medical products company experiencing rapid industry growth that has decided to use venturing to exploit it. The third, mobile communications giant Nokia, operates in a growth industry which is, perhaps, beginning to plateau out. Nokia has in response placed a business creation engine at the heart of its corporate strategy.

Shell

Shell is a global energy firm with four divisions – Exploration & Production (E&P – upstream), Oil Products (downstream), Renewables, and Chemicals. Each of these divisions has its own HQ with autonomous local operating companies sitting under them.

The energy business has two important features. The first is its scale and lengthy time horizons. When, for example, the government of Angola sold parcels of land with drilling rights, each cost in the low hundreds of millions of dollars. Gas plants take several years to build, and it took Shell decades to negotiate gas concessions in Nigeria. Second, there is an ever-present need to discover new sources for existing forms of energy and to keep an eye on new forms. Gas and oil exploration continues, while renewable forms of energy such as wind, biomass, solar and hydrogen may eventually build a substantial market share.

The company has a long history of strategic renewal and growth. It moved quickly into Liquefied Natural Gas over 25 years ago when it developed a cooling technology that enabled economic transportation. The next big challenge is new technology to permit the use of hybrid gas–liquid forms of gas, and Shell has recently built its first gas–liquid plant in Malaysia. The long-term challenge is renewable energy. According to a senior executive: 'These are the energies of the future. Our long-range scenarios suggest that this should assume prime importance somewhere between 2020 and 2050. Our strategic aim in Renewables at the moment is to build an initial capability so that we are ready to scale-up when the picture becomes clearer.'

As a result, Shell has developed advanced capabilities in investment planning. The E&P division, for instance, uses a well-established process for developing new oil acreage. Indeed, because exploration is financially riskier than development, the division has to use a different evaluation system for exploration to prevent all its investment going into development. The division also waits patiently for new country openings and is used to each task involving different sets of people. The executive says, 'In E&P, venturing is part of business renewal. We don't even see it as venturing in the classic sense of the term, because doing new things is intrinsic to our business.'

According to this executive, 'We spend tens of millions per year on planning that combines bottom-up and top-down perspectives. The E&P Global Challenge process filters projects a bit like a university. We use a ranking system and make sure conflicts of interest are avoided through independent peer reviews. If divisional executives endorse a project then it goes to E&P's managing committee and then to the CMD [Shell's Committee of Managing Directors, of which Shell's CEO is Chairman] for integration into the top-down view. They decide how much to invest in aggregate and select a portfolio of projects annually.'

Shell also operates another venturing programme – Gamechanger – to develop young, risky ideas which cannot compete on scale with business extension projects in the annual investment process. According to another executive, 'Gamechanger is a mindset. It has a powerful coalition behind it and is now entrenched. Gamechanger is funded through a divisional budget charged to the operating companies as part of the annual budget deal between them. Rules govern how projects are picked up by one of a number of units, and how bridge funding is secured to keep the business alive while waiting. Basically, a new venture needs an internal sponsor.'

Shell ran a separate E-Initiatives unit for 2 years to adapt the retail end of the company to the Internet. The unit functioned at arms-length from the operational mindset of its Oil Products division, and consisted of both business creation and venture capital. 'We did it as a centralized initiative to give the Internet a high profile within the firm and to create new skills and expertise,' says an executive. Once the unit had done its job it was reintegrated back into Shell Consumer, part of Oil Products.

What can we learn from Shell? We have seen that it uses business creation in a variety of places within the firm as a strategic technique to exploit and adapt to technological, economic and environmental change. The short answer is that Shell's supportive organizational structures and financial procedures make business creation routine.

Dispersed business creation capability

Through Gamechanger, Shell has successfully pushed business creation out from its corporate centre, beyond its divisional centres, and out to the company as a whole so that, according to the executive who completed our business creation audit, there are four places an idea can go for finance and development. To do this, it has designed structures to mitigate operational bias against business creation, such as temporarily creating E-Initiatives outside its natural Oil Products home and setting up Shell Technology Ventures to act as an agent for bringing promising new technologies into operational use.

Venturing is so well entrenched at Shell that executives we have interviewed think that business creation is nearly invulnerable to management change. Significantly, even though the company shut its E-Initiatives venture unit in Summer 2002, this made little difference to the status of business creation as one of the firm's principal business development techniques.

Incorporating business creation into investment planning

Shell has also embedded business creation into its investment planning practices. This is significant for three reasons. First, the fact that it has rigorous procedures in the first place means that business creation is much easier than it would have been had those procedures not existed. Business creation for Shell is therefore not fundamentally different from any other investment. Second, business creation has become part of the overall investment activity at the firm, meaning that it is insulated from short-term financial pressure. As we have seen throughout the book, this pressure is one of the primary causes of the death of business creation in the *Focused* firm. Third, business creation has benefited from, and been driven by, the long time horizons at Shell.

Becton Dickinson

Becton Dickinson and Company (BD) is a leading player in the medical products industry, manufacturing a variety of products including syringes, drug-delivery systems and diagnostic tests. Founded in 1897 as an importer of thermometers, BD began manufacturing its own thermometers in the US within 10 years, and gradually diversified into related medical products. Over the last decade it has grown from $2.4 billion to $3.8 billion in revenues (FY 2001) and from $200 million to $400 million net profits. The secret of the company's steady growth, according to

CEO Edward J. Ludwig, is that, 'most of the things we've become good at we didn't necessarily invent from scratch. We are great innovators and adapters.'

A key new product was the 'safety syringe', which offered additional protection to health care workers who could come in contact with patient blood but which cost three times as much as standard syringes. Safety syringes, or advanced protection devices, had sold in small quantities for years, and BD decided to invest heavily in their development. In 1998 a coalition of nurses, unions and insurance companies managed to get California to adopt a law mandating their use. This was followed by the adoption of national legislation. In November 2000 President Clinton signed the Needle-stick Safety and Prevention Act, which required all medical providers to convert to advanced protection devices by mid-2001. To date, BD has invested over $500 million in the safety products arena. The risk BD took has paid off and the company's revenues from advanced protection devices have risen by over $500 million.

BD undertook a review of its growth strategy in the late 1990s, driven by the usual pressures on companies to grow and by its experience in the advanced protection market. The Chairman of the board at that time, Clateo Castellini, decided to encourage a broader view of innovation by integrating corporate research, business development and strategic planning. All three functions were placed under the management of one executive and were to be driven by a strategic plan dictating both the direction of invest-ment and the methods for selecting projects.

■   *BD Technologies* was created out of the old BD corporate research centre. Researchers were tutored in business princi-ples and were taught to think about creating a business from the start of a research programme. Researchers were partnered early on with Business Development and Strategic Planning to create early business plans. BD's business development groups helped to identify and attract key partners early in the programmes.

■   An *external incubator programme* was started, resident at BD Technologies, whose purpose is to incubate small firms with technology complementary to BD's internal research. The programme provides BD researchers close contact with entrepreneurs and potential lead users of advanced technologies. An example is Merix Biosciences, which is developing novel cancer vaccines. BD is developing advanced devices and methods for delivering vaccines that it believes will be helpful to Merix and others in the vaccine market in the future.

- *BD Ventures* is a venture capital programme that invests in early stage companies in areas of strategic interest to BD. One example is Novocell, a diabetes therapy company. BD has a minority equity stake and a development agreement with Novocell.

These three groups report to Vince Forlenza, SVP Technology, Strategy and Development, who also manages the company's process for reviewing all strategies either from the businesses or from his own group. In addition to Forlenza, the review board is made up of the CEO, the CFO, the Corporate Medical Director, and the Presidents of BD's three major businesses.

Visibility of CEO support

The BD CEO initiated venturing during the 'safety syringe' experience and operates a system of open debate with the full participation of the senior leaders of the company. Members of the review committee are expected to act on behalf of the company and not just from the perspective of their function or business. The consequence is that attitudes to about venturing have changed from 'that's not BD' to 'we can do this!'

Central funding, divisional organization

The BD corporate centre funded the initial programmes, which were kept small until real progress could be demonstrated to a sceptical company. Now, Vince Forlenza's group provides the feasibility funding for the ventures. Once initial feasibility of the platform technology has been demonstrated, a division is asked to provide a portion of early stage application work. This begins to build commitment from the businesses more quickly than waiting until full-scale development begins.

Venturing is strategy driven

R & D, venture capital, strategic planning and business creation are organized together under the same management. Venturing is driven by BD's strategic plan and the plan is influenced by BD's venturing. It is an iterative process fundamentally driven by the portfolio of opportunities.

Nokia

Nokia has developed a highly sophisticated approach to business creation. In 1998 the company recognized the need to look beyond its existing products and technologies for growth, and it created Nokia Ventures Organization (NVO), a separate business area headed by company president Pekka Ala-Pietilä.

As we described in Chapter 4, NVO is complex. It consists of three venture units that invest in different types of opportunities (Nokia Venture Partners, Nokia Early Stage Technology, New Growth Business), a future orientated group called Insight and Foresight, and two fully-fledged but small businesses with their own P & L – Nokia Internet Communications and Nokia Home Communications. These latter two businesses emerged from the venturing process, and remain in NVO while they are relatively small and their future unclear. Rather than repeat the description provided in Chapter 4, it is more interesting to home in on the elements of NVO that we believe mark it out as an *Integrated* mode company.

NVO is a strategic priority for the company

NVO features prominently in all company publications, the President of the company runs it, and links with the other parts of the company are strong. Unlike most companies that do their best to hide the losses associated with their business creation activities, Nokia actually highlights them. Take a look at the annual report –

there are only three business units: Nokia Mobile Communications (handsets), Nokia Networks (infrastructure) and Nokia Ventures Organization. The NVO numbers are there in black and white: 2001 revenues of €585 million, and losses of €855 million. The fact that NVO lost money is irrelevant. It is exactly what we would expect from a unit that is investing in the future growth of Nokia. What is interesting about this line item in the annual report is both the amount of money invested (and this is in addition to R & D in the business units and Nokia Research centre) and also the fact that the company is prepared to report the figure.

Each venture unit has a clear objective

It may sound confusing to have three different units within NVO each investing in new businesses, but in fact it is the opposite. By having three units, each one is forced to develop clear priorities and criteria, and each develops a way of working that suits the sort of opportunities it backs. For example, Nokia Early Stage Technology (NEST) fund was created to provide a vehicle for developing ideas that New Growth Businesses (NGB) saw as having marginal strategic fit for Nokia. It therefore decided to spin its portfolio companies out as new entities that Nokia would retain the option of buying back, an approach that would not have worked in NGB.

The model is continuously evolving

Two stand-alone businesses – Nokia Internet Communications and Nokia Home Communications – emerged from NVO and will no doubt be moved out of NVO when the time is right. NEST spun-off from NGB. NGB has several businesses in its pipeline which will either become business units within NVO or independent business units. These sorts of changes happen all the time. Given that the entire structure is only 4 years old, it is remarkable how much it has already evolved.

There is a high level of self-criticism

In interviewing the executives running NVO, one observes a remarkable level of humility and self-criticism, considering how successful they have been. The head of one unit commented that, 'we have been too conservative in our investments in recent years'. Another said that, 'we have yet to develop a satisfactory vehicle for taking in early stage ideas from the outside'. One senses, too, an active interest in understanding how other companies make business creation work.

Nokia undoubtedly has its detractors as well. Some have commented that Nokia can only afford to invest so much in business creation because of its highly profitable mobile-handsets business. Others argue that it is simply too soon to call NVO a success. These points have some validity but, on current evidence, Nokia is head-and-shoulders above most of its telecoms peers in its current performance and its apparent ability to shape the future of its industry.

BUILDING AN *INTEGRATED* CAPABILITY

Shell, Becton Dickinson and Nokia are all interesting cases for different reasons. As we have shown in Chapters 3 and 4, the appropriate business creation model depends on both the underlying capabilities and the opportunity set, and in addition there are a host of industry-specific factors that prevent any particular 'best practice' model from being copied *in toto*. Nonetheless, there are a number of common themes that emerge from these and other companies we have studied. In the final part of this chapter we pull out what we see as the core imperatives for a company that wants to develop an *Integrated* business creation capability, with brief examples of each.

Embed the business creation capability in the line organization

A consistent theme in this book has been the idea that business creation can take place anywhere. *Integrated* companies recognize this, and they actively seek out ways of tapping into the latent creativity of their entire employee base. Roche Diagnostics offers an excellent example. CEO Heino von Prondzynski says, 'There are 17000 people in the company. Somewhere the new idea is there waiting to come out.' But a single unitary system is risky, and von Prondzynski is focused on decentralizing venturing across Roche Diagnostics' operations. Decentralizing into multiple units offers benchmarking and competition, and this allows business creation to be pushed down to divisions and business units. The Shell example shows how a firm with multiple units can *Emphasize* and *Ease* business creation in different parts of its operation as it sees fit. Further, business creation, as with many capabilities, lies in the heads of its practitioners. The more widely dispersed these practitioners are within the line structure of the firm, the more likely the firm is to take advantages of opportunities within its core business rather than look at relatively frivolous businesses at the fringe.

There are two different ways of embedding business creation in the line organization. The first, which we can call the *multi-focal* model, involves the continued use of venture units but with close links between them and corporate strategy. Nokia is perhaps the best example of this, and other companies including Shell, Unilever and Ericsson also have two or more discrete venture units. The second is the *dispersed* model in which business creation is embedded into the responsibilities of the line managers. We mentioned Hewlett Packard earlier as an example of a company that had taken this route, and 3M also adopts this approach. Both require the firm to enforce financial separation, as we see below.

Build visibility and legitimacy company-wide around the importance of business creation

This is an obvious and important point, yet it still deserves emphasis. Unless the venture unit or the business creation initiative has clear support from the top of the company, it is unlikely to get off the ground. Venture unit managers talk in terms of the 'air cover' they get from their superiors, and they appreciate the legitimacy they gain from being seen to be worth the time of the top executives. All of the successful venturing initiatives we have seen in recent years, including Nokia, Ericsson, Shell, Roche and BD, began at the top.

However, while top executive sponsorship is absolutely crucial to business creation, it is still not enough. The risk of a venture unit being associated too closely with one executive is that it gets killed-off when the executive in question leaves the company. To varying degrees we saw this happen in Lucent, Royal & Sun Alliance and British Airways. So for business creation to exist as an *Integrated* capability, it has to be institutionalized within the company in such a way that it can withstand the departure of its key sponsor. 3M and HP have certainly achieved this level of legitimacy as have Shell and BD, but even Nokia, notwithstanding its current successes, has yet to show that its Ventures Organization can survive a change in leadership.

A firm can achieve this level of legitimacy through a mixture of practical success and persistent communication from the CEO. The message here is to generate some successes and make sure that they are widely broadcast again and again until it sinks in. Companies such as 3M did not create their entrepreneurial culture overnight; they developed it over several decades. In terms of executive support, the fact that Nokia Ventures Organization is headed by Nokia's CEO proves that business creation is a strategic priority for the firm. Shell's continuing Gamechanger programme displays significant commitment.

We have shown that *Ad Hoc* firms shovel the risks of venturing on to their employees and that *Focused* firms assume this risk and then reduce it by killing ventures more quickly and doing them more cheaply. How a firm treats employees who have worked in a failed venture sends a strong signal across the company about business creation. An *Integrated* company understands that a venture may fail for business reasons rather than because its managers and staff bungle it. Such tolerance for understandable failure shows that business creation is mainstream.

Create a systematic approach that will survive in a downturn

This point is related to the previous one but merits special consideration in the current business environment. Just as the *Integrated* mode transcends the tenure of a particular chief executive, it also transcends the particular stages of the business cycle. Writing this book in 2002, we see countless examples of companies that have killed-off their venture units as a knee-jerk reaction to the losses they made in venturing and their broader financial difficulties. However, we also see companies that have wisely retained their capability and are continuing to invest through the downturn, when prices are reasonable and there is less competition from other investors. This list of companies includes corporate venture capital investors such as Intel, Siemens and France Telecom, as well as companies investing in internal opportunities such as Nokia, Ericsson, BAT, Shell, BD and Sainsbury's.

Flexibility is an important feature of a systematic approach. In both the Nokia and Shell examples in this chapter we showed how these two firms are constantly evolving the way they undertake business creation and where in the firm they do it. In particular, business creation staff need to move around to keep themselves fresh and to bring skills to parts of the firm where they are most needed.

Foster an entrepreneurial culture in the company

Most large company cultures are pretty oppressive. Even when they claim to be open-minded, they typically create systems and structures that obstruct the progress of all but the most committed entrepreneurs. The *Integrated* mode, on the other hand, demands a broad level of acceptance, even enthusiasm, for business creation – a far cry from the prevailing culture in most large companies.

How does a company change its culture from oppressive to open-minded? There are no simple answers, and the issue is covered far better elsewhere. However, in the context of our model, it is worth acknowledging an important point: that the *Focused* mode, in the form of a venture unit, often acts as a catalyst for wider change in the company. Consider again the case of Roche Diagnostics, where Heino von Prondzynski believes that the enduring value of its venture programme will be to create a complete change in organization culture, so that staff throughout the company have commercial skills and can discuss concepts such as new business models. Other companies told us similar stories. Brightstar was seen as a catalyst for change in BT's traditional R & D labs, and in Marks & Spencer, the venture unit promoted a new way of thinking and a capability to act quickly, which were important ingredients in the company's overall transformation.

It is important, therefore, to create a positive feedback loop, in which a successful venture unit fosters the development of a more entrepreneurial culture, which in turn leads to more venturing activities and the success of the venture unit. In his book on the need for business creation, *Leading the Revolution*, Gary Hamel uses the phrase 'market in money, ideas and people' to sum up his idea that large firms should bring the market inside. We think of successful business creation more as taking place within a managed business development market – after all, there are limits to how much business creation a firm can do.

Successful markets are transparent, neutral and open. In Chapters 7 and 8 we showed how the venture unit can adopt behaviours and attitudes, such as transparency, openness and neutrality, to increase the flow of good ideas from all sources. Such behaviours and attitudes, from management as well as from the venture unit, are central to a company's success in fostering an entrepreneurial culture that mimics the actions, and brings the benefits, of the market.

Create networks with venture capitalists and small-firm communities

Effective business creation is as much about managing external networks as internal processes. It is widely recognized in the information technology and biotechnology industries, for example, that small firms are a key source of technological innovations, and that part of the business creation challenge is to find ways of linking up with them during their early stages of development. This involves creating relationships directly with these companies, but also working with the venture capital community who have the best access to the 'deal flow'.

What is the best way of developing these external networks? The most successful companies, such as Intel Capital, France Telecom (through its Innovacom venture capital unit) and Nokia have taken an incremental approach, first of investing as a limited partner in a venture capital fund, then co-investing with venture capitalists, and then taking the lead. Jon Hanley, the head of Lucent Venture Partners, described his approach:

> We courted the venture capitalists, who split two ways – some gave us second round strategic partnerships, nice but not really what we were looking for; others took us at our word, and threw us a bone in early stage – perhaps a small investment opportunity alongside theirs. But we acted on these opportunities, and genuinely added value, so the venture capitalists started to figure out that they were serious. We eventually got to know a few venture capital partners in depth, and built up personal relationships with them. They now bring us early stage stuff, but it is hard work.

Michael Pearson, who runs Strategic Ventures at Lloyds TSB, reports that he too has learned from venture capitalists: 'I gained in four areas – governance, gating funding, the need for flexibility as the venture unfolds and business models change, and the importance of the management team. The result was that when a formal programme of venturing started at Lloyds TSB I had a head start.' Nick Basing of Unilever provides another perspective: 'No matter how smart the people inside the company, there are always smarter people outside.'

Venture capitalists provide a valuable and often uncomfortable perspective on potential investments for the corporation. Their view is usually shorter term and tends to emphasize financial benefit to the exclusion of strategic benefit. However, their inclusion in the investment process is like an effective but often bad-tasting medicine.

Embed venturing in the strategic management process

We have commented previously on the syndrome of business development projects arriving in deal form and being given the nod by a single executive on a yes/no basis. This leads to the kind of business planning that results when opportunity and execution are muddled and the writer is simply justifying a decision that has already been made.

This situation can be avoided through two safeguards. The first is that business creation be linked to all of the other strategic activities in the company, including venture capital, mergers and acquisitions, and strategic planning. Philips, for example, co-located its venture unit with its alliances and M & A units, on the premise that they represent complementary business development techniques. Many of the *Focused* firms that we feature have also organized business creation with strategy and the rest of business development, among them Roche and Lloyds TSB. All *Integrated* firms, by definition, organize themselves in this way.

The second and more important safeguard is that business creation be strategy-led. This comes about when companies use strategic fit and strategic importance as the final decision criteria they use when selecting ventures for investment, all other criteria having been satisfied. As we have seen, BD drives all its business development activities from its strategic plan, while in the late 1990s Sainsbury's moved away from what one executive there calls a 'here's a good idea, let's spend some money on it' syndrome to operating a fully-fledged and widely-communicated strategic management agenda. Now, according to the executive, 'anything to do with venturing has to support the strategic agenda'.

Keep financially separate

In Chapter 4 we showed how the *Integrated* firm moves between *Emphasize* and *Ease* on the business creation model and matches its level of relevant business creation activity to the level of business opportunities available. This naturally does not mean that large firms should carry out every single business creation project that has answered all the investment criteria that we outlined in Chapter 6. Nor does it mean that we recommend pursuing all projects that have an NPV of above zero for a suitable risk-adjusted discount rate. We recognize that firms have a natural capacity for investment as against operations. This capacity is a function of the firm's borrowing capacity, the relative demand of the financial markets for earnings as against growth, management time and a host of other factors. By *Emphasize* we mean that when suitable opportunities for growth or renewal arrive then firms should direct more of their investment capacity to business creation.

At Shell, the Committee of Managing Directors determines the firm's overall level of investment per year. In order to do this, Shell has to manage its investment activities separately, in a financial sense, from its operations activities, although of course it organizes them together. Becton Dickinson, as we saw, goes nearly as far by funding its ventures centrally but organizing them locally. Nokia reports its NVO profit and loss separately in its financial results.

For management, therefore, this financial separation provides the means to:

- Strategically scale business creation to match the firm's investment capacity and the opportunities that it faces.

- Report venturing activities separately, so that analysts and investors can distinguish between operating and investment activities and place a separate value on each.

- Place venturing and ventures within the line organization, if appropriate, without incurring resistance from P & L-focused executives.

- Mix investment and operating activities within the firm without the short-time horizons of the latter driving out the former.

In our view financial separation is the single most important measure that the management of a large firm can take to provide an environment in which business creation can thrive.

CONCLUSION

In this chapter we have made three points about how to develop an *Integrated* approach to venturing:

- In the *Integrated* mode, business creation is a dispersed capability, rather than something that is held only in a venture unit. This makes it less fragile, but there is also a risk that the capability gets spread too thin.

- There are many companies that exhibit some of the characteristics of the *Integrated* mode, including Shell, Becton Dickinson and Nokia, each of which is profiled. But each of these three companies uses a different approach.

- There are seven distinct attributes to an *Integrated* capability: embedding in the line organization; company-wide visibility and CEO support; an entrepreneurial culture; networks of relationships with venture capitalists and small-firm communities; use of a systematic approach; embedding in the strategic management process; and financial separation from P & L-focused operating units.

Afterword

THE CHIEF EXECUTIVE AS ARCHITECT

In this final couple of pages, we briefly turn our attention to the role of the Chief Executive Officer in the process of business creation. In theory, one can envision a relatively limited role for the CEO, because the essence of a 'system' for business creation is that it is depersonalized. In reality, it is clear that he or she makes all the difference – in putting the venturing activity together in the first place, in supporting it through hard times, and in providing the sense of direction to the collective business creation efforts of the employees. Ultimately, the system is a reflection of the CEO and his or her belief in business creation.

However, this reflection can be more or less intense. At one extreme there are CEOs such as Bill Gates, Larry Ellison and Richard Branson who *are* the business creation engines of their respective companies. These executives take personal responsibility for seeking out new opportunities, building relationships with other companies, and committing large sums of money to the next 'big thing'. At the other extreme, there are the quiet CEOs who let their system and culture do the talking. 3M, for example, has an enviable reputation for its ability to build new businesses, but its CEOs from William McKnight to Desi Desimone have typically shunned the spotlight. Between these two extremes, the CEO plays a dual role, sometimes standing back because the system is running well, and sometimes taking a more active and decisive role when he or she believes that intervention is necessary.

In the course of this research, we encountered many CEOs who believe strongly in business creation as the prime driver of renewal and growth, as well as many others who preferred the quick fix of the acquisition. The person who best exemplifies our belief in the importance of business creation is Sir Peter Davis, who has had an illustrious career in UK industry, as Chairman of Reed Elsevier, Group Chief Executive of Prudential plc and CEO of Sainsbury's. Davis has, of course, done his share of cost-cutting, downsizing, partnering and acquiring, but a common theme in his executive roles has been the importance of business creation. His contrasting approaches at Prudential Insurance and Sainsbury's are worth highlighting.

PETER DAVIS: SERIAL BUSINESS CREATOR

Davis became CEO of Prudential in 1995, which at the time was seen as a slow-moving and old-fashioned company in an industry undergoing rapid change. Davis made a number of acquisitions to take the company into new areas of the insurance and invest-ment business, but his central thrust was the creation of Egg, an Internet and telephone bank that gave the company direct access to customers.

Egg was launched in 1999 as a completely separate business. While it occupied adjacent premises to the rest of Prudential in central London, it operated in a more informal and flexible way. For example, within days of launching the business, Egg had to more than double the size of its call centre operation to cope with customer demand. Its staff managed to get the new capacity up and running within 4 days. In contrast, Davis observed, 'Prudential would not have found the forms in 4 days'.

Egg rapidly became the UK's biggest Internet bank. There were also some interesting spillovers into the rest of the Prudential. Some people complained about the special attention shown to Egg, but there was also pride in what they as a company had achieved. Some individuals moved over to Egg. To those who stayed in the traditional businesses, Davis challenged them to learn from Egg and become more flexible and innovative themselves.

The Egg launch was a classic example of successful business creation through separation. Davis recognized that trying to build the business inside the existing Prudential structure would have killed it, so he created a separate entity and gave it the resources and freedom it needed to succeed.

Davis was recruited to the CEO position at Sainsbury's in 2000, when the company was in a poor state of health. He had worked there earlier in his career and so knew the business, but he found himself leading a company that had lost its way. It had under-invested in its core supermarket business for years and its image had been blurred through a number of poorly-received marketing campaigns. Tesco, and increasingly Walmart through its acquisition of Asda, were now seen as the market leaders.

To get the company back on track, Davis started by reverting to basics, first cutting back on a number of non-core areas, then by pursuing a big investment programme in the core supermarket business. Then followed a process that he called 'Reinvent' which essentially involved looking for new business opportunities around the existing customer base – a mobile phone business, power, joint ventures with Boots and Unilever, a second-generation reward programme called 'Nectar', and many other projects. It is too soon to be sure of the results, but Reinvent is already beginning to show some positive returns.

While its purpose was to create new businesses, Reinvent was *not* a venture unit. Davis felt that a venture unit was the last thing Sainsbury's needed while it was trying to regain its focus. Instead, he saw Reinvent as a process of developing new business ventures tied closely and explicitly to the strategic planning process. Importantly, he brought with him enormous credibility from his time at Reed and Prudential, and so quickly gained support for his ideas.

Davis' contrasting approaches at Prudential and Sainsbury's underscore two points. First, the business creation mode you adopt depends on the situation in which you find yourself – the assets, systems and cultures of the company, as well as its opportunities. Second, it highlights the important role of the CEO in defining the business creation agenda. Some CEOs are known for cost-cutting and downsizing (Al Dunlap, former CEO of Sunbeam). Some are known for selling off peripheral businesses and focusing on the core (George Simpson, former CEO of Marconi). Others are best known for their acquisitions (Chris Gent at Vodafone and Jean Marie Messier at Vivendi). A few are known as business creators – mostly in a single company (Michael Eisner at Disney), but occasionally in more than one. Davis is the best example we know of a 'serial business creator', and as such he is emblematic of the theme of this book.

PERSEVERING WITH BUSINESS CREATION

In *Inventuring* we have encouraged companies to adopt an integrated and firm-wide approach to business creation but, as will be clear by now, the process of developing the required capabilities is far from straightforward.

The *Integrated* mode of business creation is difficult to live with. There are always forces within large companies that get in the way of business creation – 'nay sayers' who vote down exciting new projects, cost-cutters who trim down investment budgets, and cynics who resist anything new. So, an *Integrated* approach to business creation can include periods of running fast and others of standing still.

However, this should not deter you. The rewards for success are large, and the process is invigorating. In one company we spoke to, the venture unit manager told us of a 57-year-old mother-of-two who had been involved in a venture project. The woman observed that working in the venture had been, 'the thing she had been most proud of in her entire life.' This was a life-changing event for her, and equally it was something that her colleagues and her entire organization drew value from.

The financial and strategic contribution of the technique to the imperatives of growth and renewal are now clear. Business creation is cheaper and less risky than acquisition and more suited to core activities than venture capital, and the system that we have outlined makes it accessible for any firm. The technique of business creation is valuable and feasible, and a necessary tool for today's CEO.

Index

Notes

Kudu (Chapters 1 and 3), Belleron (4), Telegene (5 and 12), Portisco (6), Arcus (10), Decadia (11), Pentameter (11) and Cyntec (13) are disguised examples and are not included in the index.

Topics related to the firm are generally to be found under 'Business creation', and those related to ventures under entries starting 'Venture'.

Other books from McGraw-Hill

10 Things That Keep CEOs Awake – And How to Put Them to Bed
By COFFEY
Price: £19.99
ISBN: 0077099893

Coffey and a team of expert coaches address the primary concerns of today's CEOs. Each chapter sets its subject in context, explains a specific challenge, defines a set of desired results and shows how the client was guided to achieving them.

Manager's Guide to Self-Development
By PEDLER, BURGOYNE and BOYDELL
Price: £19.99
ISBN: 0077098307

This book is designed as a self-development programme for managers seeking to develop skills such as mental agility, creativity, social skills and emotional resilience.

Tools For Success – A Manager's Guide
By TURNER
Price: £19.99
ISBN: 0077098706

A one-stop guide to all the essential management tools, which will help you to develop the performance of your team and your organization. The book is set out in an easy-to-read, two-page format with clear descriptions of the tools and how to use them. All the tools have been tried and tested in real situations by internationally recognized companies.

Successful Mergers, Acquisitions and Strategic Alliances – How to Bridge Corporate Culture
By GANCEL, RAYNAUD and ROGERS
Price: £26.99
ISBN: 0077098757

A unique and pragmatic diagnostic model – the Culture Bridging Fundamentals (CBF©), which provides practical help to senior executives and their advisors. It is based on 18 years' experience consulting with Fortune 500 companies. The result is a proven approach to achieving the positive predicted outcomes of an alliance.

Recruiting Excellence – An Insider's Guide to Sourcing Top Talent
By GROUT
Price: £19.99
ISBN: 0077099680

An insider's guide to identifying, attracting, selecting, motivating and retaining top talent: the guide reveals the strategies, tactics and practical procedures that maximises the people-power driving your business to success.

Mastering Strategy – Insights from the World's Greatest Leaders and Thinkers
By RIGSBY
Price: £18.99
ISBN: 0071402861

The best strategies from ground-breaking CEOs, thought-leading academics, and top companies combined to form a blueprint to strategic business thinking and planning.

Art and Discipline of Strategic Leadership
By FREEDMAN
Price: £21.99
ISBN: 007141066X

An integrated approach to strategy setting and execution for managers at all levels, from a senior executive of one of the world's most respected consulting companies, Kepner-Tregoe.

Leadershock ... And How to Triumph Over It By HICKS
Price: £14.99
ISBN: 0071408010

Short, provocative guide to contrarian leadership principles by the co-author of 'What It Takes to Be Happy'.

Winning The Merger Endgame – A Playbook for Profiting from Industry Consolidation
By DEANS
Price: £29.99
ISBN: 007140998X

Based on research drawn from A.T. Kearney's landmark study, this book presents a game plan for how executives can develop the strategies necessary to accomplish successful mergers.